The Families Of
Moir And Byres

Andrew John Mitchell Gill

Alpha Editions

This Edition Published in 2021

ISBN: 9789354369506

Design and Setting By
Alpha Editions
www.alphaedis.com
Email – info@alphaedis.com

PREFACE.

At first the intention was to give an account merely of the family of Moir-Byres of Tonley, together with short notices of the families they are related to by marriage, &c. In the search for information on the various heads, so much was got, connected more or less remotely with these families, that I thought it a pity not to utilise what had cost so much time and trouble to gather together. It is much to be regretted that admission has not been had to the deeds and papers of the various families; and also, through absence from home, I have been unable to exhaust several valuable sources of information, such as the Burgess Registers and Sheriff Court Records, &c. of Aberdeen.

It will be seen that the surname of Moir or More can fairly rank as one of the oldest in the county of Aberdeen, even without entering into the debateable question of Ranald or Reginald More, Chamberlain of Scotland, being progenitor of the *Moirs*, as well as of the *Muirs*, who, as will be seen at page 3, had large grants of land in Aberdeenshire in 1328.

As landowners, however—with the exception of Patrick More de Belhelvie, in 1467, page 4—few of them appear before the seventeenth and eighteenth centuries, and previous to that period the heads of most of the different families (doubtless all originally of the same stock) seem to have been mostly substantial Burgesses of Bon-Accord.

Of the gallant and brave Moirs of Stoneywood there were only four generations—John Moir of Kermuck, afterwards of Stoneywood, *the founder*— keen, honest, and shrewd, as became his good Burgess ancestry. He was succeeded by his son, James Moir, II. of Stoneywood, a learned and gallant gentleman, for fifteen years M.P. for his county, whose picture, attributed to Scougal, is in the Tonley collection. His son was James Moir, III. of Stoneywood, the brave and staunch supporter of his Prince, who, along with Lord Lewis Gordon and his kinsman, Moir of Lonmay, was amongst the most important of Charles Stuart's supporters in Aberdeenshire. He was succeeded by his equally good and brave son, James Moir, IV. and last of Stoneywood, the tried friend of his unfortunate Prince. With this worthy son of worthy sires ended the male line of the gallant Stoneywoods, whose representatives through the female line are the Skenes of Rubislaw. Lands and houses pass away, and the place which knew them knows them no more.

Of the " broad acres " owned by the name of Moir in Aberdeenshire, only two families of the surname hold estates in the county—viz., Moir-Byres of Tonley, whose lands came to them through the Byres family, and the old family of Moir of

Scotstown, who have owned that property for at
least eight generations, and who were much connected with the University and Old Town of Aberdeen. Its present representative, William Moir, is
a Lieutenant in the 18th Hussars, and will, I hope,
uphold "the auld hous," and add to, instead of
diminish the family inheritance.

Moir of Invernettie had aspired to "founding a
family," and registered arms on his own account;
but his line became extinct before the parent stem
of Stoneywood, and Invernettie reverted to that
family.

Of the loyal Moirs of Lonmay, the son of the
Prince's brave supporter sold the estate and bought
New Grange, in Forfarshire, which was, however,
soon again parted with. The representative of this
family, Captain Moir, was ignominiously hanged in
London (see page 78).

William Moir, M.P., of Hilton, although also
wishful to "found a house," and between 1672-8
registering arms, endures only a few years; and in
1682 there is another Laird, and even the name of
his estate is changed.

Moir of Barnes, out of a family of four sons and
nine daughters, appears at his decease to have only
left eight daughters, his co-heiresses, whose hus-
bands, no doubt, carefully and quickly divided his
estate of the Abergeldie Moirs. I have no particulars excepting of their cadet, "Moir of Otterburn," (for the account of which family I am in-
debted, along with a great deal of other most useful

information, to the kindness of Mr. R. R. Stodart,
Lyon Depute), of which house there were five Lairds;
but in 1765 their estates were also sold.

From pages 84 to 96 will be found a notice of *all
the Moirs*, extracted from the Register of St.
Nicholas from 1570 to 1700, and although many of
the entries obviously belong to families whose
genealogy is given in the body of the work, the
author thought it better, as he has had no access to
family papers, &c., to leave them, in most cases, in
this register, rather than guess at their proper place
in the various genealogies.

Of the Tonley Moirs we have first, at page 11,
the careful and canny burgess of Aberdeen, Andrew
Moir of Overhill, who is able to give his large
family by two wives each a comfortable "set-out"
in the world. His eldest son likewise, Andrew
Moir, follows a country life, and devotes himself to
agriculture. No doubt his wife, the Laird of Thornton's daughter, brings with her a suitable dowry.
He is thus able to place his sons comfortably in the
world, and to give each of his four daughters such a
tocher as will not decrease their attractions in the
eyes of a fond husband. The eldest son of the last
couple, the Reverend Andrew Moir, was for nearly
thirty years the minister of Ellon. By his well-born
wife, Jean Forbes, of the family of Waterton, he
had, with other issue—

The Reverend George Moir, his heir, who was
for fifty-five years the much-loved and respected
minister of Peterhead; his wife, Martha Byres,

[*Page v. of Preface.*]

It is a mistake to designate Patrick Byres of Tonley as a Roman Catholic, he being in fact a Presbyterian.—ED.

Two of this fine couple's sons married their cousins, who were sisters ; but John Moir, the younger brother, married the elder sister, Catherine Byres, whose descendants, as shown in the sequel, now hold Tonley ; while Janet Byres, the younger sister, married the elder brother, James Moir, M.D., and their son Patrick Moir-Crane is the present head of this branch of the Moir family, and heir-presumptive to Tonley.

Of the family of Byres, I am inclined to think that Thomas de Byres, who in 1392 owned lands in Edinburgh, was the real progenitor of the race, that the surname was assumed from the lands of Byres, in the parish and county of Haddington, and that the Hungarian-Franco story is exceedingly mythical. Of the house of Coates, its founder undoubtedly was the prosperous and talented trader, and good citizen of Edinburgh, John Byres, born in 1569, who was of the same stock as the Byres of the counties of Haddington and Lanark, &c. (In the last century, a branch of the family owned in 1661 the estate of Strathaven, see page 142.) By his first wife, Dame Margaret Barclay, the Laird of Coates had daughters only ; but by his second wife, Agnes Smyth, a sister of Sir John Smyth, Knight of

Groithill and King's Cramond, M.P., he had at least five sons.

John Byres, I. of Coates, was succeeded by his eldest son, the brave and gallant Sir John Byres, a devoted Loyalist, who added the estate of Warrestone to his patrimonial inheritance, and seems to have left his family in a prosperous condition.   By his wife Isobel, daughter of Sir John Auchmuty of Gosford, he had his son and heir, John Byres, III. of Coates, through whose extravagance, and it is also believed by losses in the ill-managed Darien scheme, by which his Aberdeen kinsman also suffered severely, the estates had to be sold.

That the family of Byres of Tonley are descendants of the house of Coates, I have no doubt, although as yet the connection has not been satisfactorily traced.   James Byres, a prosperous merchant of Aberdeen, was married there in 1667 to Janet Middleton, page 114.   At page 109 I hazard the suggestion that he may have been the youngest son of John Byres, I. of Coates, although I have no evidence to show that he had such a son.   However, I think it more likely that this James Byres of Aberdeen was the son of William Byres, born 1627 (called James in the family memoir), the fifth son of John Byres, I. of Coates, and Agnes Smyth, and that this William Byres may have been a captain under Montrose.

Robert Byres (the son of James Byres and Janet Middleton) was a merchant of good standing in Holland and in Dublin, but met his death by accidental drowning in the Bay of Dublin, before he had been able to follow out his Scotch instinct of buying an estate and "founding a family." However, his widow, Jean Sandilands (and her late husband's trustees), bought in 1718 for their son, Patrick Byres, the lands and barony of "bonnie" Tonley, which have since continued to be the home of the head of the house. Patrick Byres, I. of Tonley, as shown in the text, was a zealous supporter of his Prince, was "out in the '45," remained for some time an exile in France, and his estate was all but forfeited. He registered arms in 1755, and in the patent is described as "*representative of the family of Coates*," for what reason does not appear; but the blazon was then considerably altered, and the old crest—a bee—was changed to a cock, with the motto, "Safe by his own exertions," a most appropriate motto for one who no doubt had many narrow escapes with his life. By his wife, Janet Moir (a daughter of James Moir, M.P., III. of Stoneywood), he had, with other issue, his son and heir—

James Byres, II. of Tonley, who was also a zealous Jacobite, and for some time a Captain in Lord Ogilvie's Regiment. Mr. Byres was a gentleman of great learning and culture, eminent as an antiquary, and resided for forty years at Rome. Returning from thence in 1790, he settled at Tonley, where he died unmarried in 1817. Like most men, he had his "romance." He had cherished an affection for Miss Fraser of Castle Fraser, but something came between them—"True love never

did run smooth." Neither married, and when the
lady died she left her old admirer her picture (which
is still at Tonley) and her carriage. The next Laird
was General Patrick Byres, the nephew of his predecessor (son of Robert Byres of Kincraigie, page
124, and Margaret Burnett), who, besides being a
brave soldier, was much loved as a good neighbour,
kind friend to the poor, and amiable country gentleman.

The unfortunate death of Lieutenant James Byres
of the 1st Royals (the only son of the General), who
was accidentally drowned at Allilane, ended the male
line of Byres of Tonley; after which the succession
opened to the Moir family.

In conclusion, I beg to acknowledge gratefully the
cordial assistance I have received from Mr. GEORGE
BURNETT, Lord Lyon, Mr. R. R. STODART, Lyon
Depute, Mr. W. F. SKENE, of Inverleith Row, Edin-
burgh (whose father compiled the valuable Stoney-
wood MS., which he kindly lent me), CAPTAIN
DUNBAR-DUNBAR of Sea Park, the Rev. WALTER
MACLEOD of Edinburgh, and others.

I hope that any corrections and additional information will be sent to me, addressed Isthmian Club,
12 Grafton Street, London, W., and that the portion
of a good-natured public who may be interested in
family history will look leniently on a work in which
I am assured there are many inaccuracies.

A. J. MITCHELL GILL.

OF THE SURNAME OF MOIR OR MORE.

By the evidence of ancient charters, the orthography of this name seems to have been so various as to occasion some difficulty in distinguishing the different families who bore it, as we find individuals of the same family promiscuously designed by the names of Moir, More, Moor, More, Mure, Muir, sometimes contracted to M', and even Moreson, Morrison, and Mureson. The name has a double origin, from Maure or Saracen, borne by foreign families in most of the continental countries of Europe, varied in accordance with the peculiar idiom of the country, and in Scotland from the Gaelic etymology, *Mohr*, big or great—allusive to remarkable size of person. Of the five entries of arms in the Lyon Office to families of the name of Moir or More in Scotland, all are connected with Aberdeenshire, and bear the three Moors' or Saracens' heads, see p. 46. The name of Morison in Scotland bears azure three Saracens' heads, conjoined in one neck proper, the faces looking to the chief dexter and sinister sides of the shield.

The family and surname of Muir is much mixed up, and often confused with, that of More or Moir. The principal family of the surname of Muir seems to have been the Muirs of Rowallan, in Ayrshire, who bear, argent, on a fesse azure, three stars or, quite different bearings from the name of Moir or More ; yet there are not wanting instances where two or more families, having the same surname, and tracing to a common ancestor, bear quite distinct arms.

A

One, if not the most ancient family of the surname of More, was that of Polkellie, in the county of Renfrew. Gilchrist More was one of the Barons who swore fealty to Edward I. in 1296. The heiress of Polkellie, Janet More, in the time of David II., married Sir Adam Muir of Rowallan.

1296.
Nisbit's
Heraldry.

The late Mr. James Skene of Rubislaw, in a valuable and most interesting MS. history by him of the " Moirs of Stoneywood " family, kindly lent me by his son, Mr. W. F. Skene, says, " Sir Gilchrist More was a descendant of the Irish O'Mores ; and that the connection appears from the grant made by Sir Gilchrist Muir of Rowallan (who was knighted at the battle of Largs) of his lands of Polkellie to his Irish kinsman, Ranald More, who had come over to assist in a contest with the Cumings, and that the O'Mores in Ireland bore as crest the Moire's head, or ' Bluidy Heid,' in allusion to the family name." He also says " several families possessing property in the Western counties of Scotland branched off at different times from that of Rowallan and Polkellie, most of whom adopted the name of Mure, although More was the original orthography used both in Ireland and Great Britain."

1263.

The Moires, Marquises of Drogheda, in Ireland, have a Moor's head, out of a coronet, for crest, and their arms have a resemblance in the charges, although not in the tinctures, to those of the family of Muir of Rowallan.

But we will now confine ourselves to the history of the Moirs or Mores in Aberdeenshire. " The introduction of the name into that county, may, with great probability, be assigned to the circumstance of the extensive possessions acquired there by Sir

Reginald More, the Chamberlain, in David II.'s Skene's MS. reign; and it is remarkable that while the families in the western counties have almost all adopted the name of Mure or Muir, those of Aberdeenshire have as uniformly retained the original orthography of More and Moir." In the older records, however, I often find the surname of the Aberdeenshire Moirs spelt also More and Moire, Moore, &c., and in a very few cases Muire and Mure.

OF THE MORES OR MOIRS OF ABER-
DEENSHIRE.

1328. Sir Adam More, witness to charter of the hospital of Turriff.—(" Antiquities of the Shire of Aberdeen," Spalding Club, vol. ii., p. 339.) Ranald or Reginald More, chamberlain of Scotland, has a charter from David II. of the lands of Formartine, Akintoir (Kintore), Aboyne, Mickle Morphie, and Converays.

1382. Johannis Mor, witness to an absolution, Canon of Aberdeen.—(" Registrum Episcopatus Aberdonensis," Spalding Club, vol. i., p. 163, &c.)

1472. Robert Moir, witness to a charter of the lands of Balmur (Balmuir), Torterstoune, Cocklaw (all in the parish of Peterhead).—(" Antiquities of the Shire of Aberdeen, vol. iii., p. 591.)

1473. Andrew More, merchant at Bruges (in France), is mentioned in a deed, Andrew Reid of Bad-

fothels (Pitfoddels), at Aberdeen, Thomas
Moir, also.—*Ibid.*, pp. 261 and 262.

Skene's MS.
1467. Patrick More de Belhelvie.⎫ " Baillie Court
1457. William Moor.   ⎬   Books of
1440. Simon More.   ⎭   Aberdeen."
1529. M' James Moir, Regent.

1539. 16th May. Andrew Moir, in the Knock, Banffshire. Witness to a charter dated at Froster-
seit.—(" Reg. of the Great Seal," vol. iii.,
p. 449).

David Moir ("Antiquities of the Shire of
Aberdeen," vol. ii., p. 262).

1550. William Moir owns a tenement of land in
the Shiprow.

1566. David Moir infeft in the lands of Braid-
haugh, Privy Council Records. And many
others that might be mentioned ; sufficient
it is to show how long the name has been in
the district. The progenitors of all of the
landed families of the name of Moir, in
Aberdeenshire, appear to have been substantial burgesses of the city of Bon-
Accord, and could the connection only now
be traced, would doubtless be found to
spring at no very distant date from a
common ancestor.

There were a good many landed families of the
surname of Moir, mostly in Aberdeenshire, in the
seventeenth and eighteenth centuries, viz., the Moirs
Skene's MS. (said to have been first designed of Ferryhill), of
Kermuck or Ellon, thereafter of Stoneywood,
amongst whose cadets I may mention Moir of
Whitehill, in Midlothian, an estate which came to
them from the Scougal family, see p. 77, afterwards

of Lonmay, in Buchan, which last estate was sold, and New Grange, in Forfarshire, bought. The Moirs of Invernettie, which estate, on the extinction of that line, reverted back to Stoneywood. The next family in importance to Stoneywood was Moir of Scotstoun, whose cadets were, so far as I know, Spittal, Denmore, and Park on Deeside. Besides these, there were Moirs of Hilton (now Turnerhall) of Abergeldie, afterwards of Otterburn, in Stirlingshire, of Barnes, &c., most of whom will be noticed afterwards.

MOIRS IN FOVERAN.

1574. 30th Novr. William Moir, in Auchloun, a farm now on the estate of Tillery.— ("Sheriff Court Records of Aberdeen, and Antiquities of the Shire of Aberdeen," Spalding Club.)

1575. Octr. Agnes Moir in Meikle Haddo.—*Ibid.*

1596. May 29. John Moir in Newburgh.—*Ibid.*

1597. 21st April. Andrew Moir, Smyth in Foveran, against Helen Fraser, tried for witchcraft. ("Miscellany of the Spalding Club," vol. i., p. 108.) In the list of "Nomina assise" (Court held at Aberdeen) occurs at p. 110, *ibid.*, the names of William Moir in Balgeirscho, and Andrew Moir, Smyth in Foveran.

Reg. of St. Nicholas, Aberdeen, 1613, 22d June, Arthur Udny—no doubt of the family of that ilk— and Janett Moir, married at Fowerane.

From Register of Baptisms, Parish of Foveran.

William Mor in Belhelvie has a son—

1. Alexander, bap. 4th Jany 1659. Witnesses, Alexander Lindsay of Many, and Alexander Lyon in Darahill.

Poll Book, vol. ii., pp. 226 and 231. Alexander Pirie in Auchnacant, in the parish of Foveran, afterwards in Meikle Tipperty, in the adjoining parish of Logie-Buchan, m^d Agnes, dau. of Andrew Moir I. of Oldmill,[1] by his first wife, see pp. 11-15 (b. 1668, Mrs. Pirie died 14th Feby 1696. Tombstone in Foveran churchyard.) Alexander Pirie was clerk and collector of the poll tax for Logie-Buchan, 1695-96. Issue—

1. Andrew, bap. 30th June 1686. Witnesses, Andrew Moir and Andrew Sutherland.
2. Jean, bap. 27th April 1688. Witnesses, Andrew Moir, child's grandfather, and Robert Moir, probably child's uncle.
3. Agnes.
4. Barbara (the four children, all mentioned on tombstone, had probably died young). The George Pirie in Savoek, who appears as a witness of the bap. of the Revd George Moir in 1679, &c.—see p. 12—had been probably a brother of Alexander's in Tipperty, and of James Pirie, who was settled at

---

[1] Andrew Moir I. of Oldmill, see p. 11, had, I think, by his first wife (with James, died young, p. 7) :—

1. Alexander, in Newtyle. See next page.
2. Gilbert, in Haddo, m^d 1st . . . and 2dly, 1681, Janet Forbes of Blackhall, p. 9.
3. Robert, in Overhill, p. 9.
1. Agnes, m^d Alexander Pirie, as above.
   And probably more children.

Irewells, in Udny parish, towards the end
of the seventeenth century, who by his first
wife, Helen Mair, was father of William
Pirie, b. in 1700—the first of the name
who settled at Orchardton in that parish—
a place his descendants resided at for
nearly two centuries ; who by his wife,
Elizabeth Laing, had Patrick Pirie, who m[d]
1st March 1778 Margaret, dau. of Alexander Smith, papermaker, Stoneywood ; and
thus begun the Piries' connection with the
paper trade, which their descendants, the
Piries of Stoneywood and Waterton, have
so ably conducted and extended. The
younger son, James Pirie, succ[d] to Orchardton, and was grandfather of the late James
Pirie, see p. 23.

Alexander Moir in Newtyle (perhaps another son
of Andrew Moir I. by his first wife).

1. Christian, bap. 30th Jan[y] 1659. Witnesses,
John Turing, in Overhills, and George
Thomson in Pitmillan.

2. Lilian, bap. 1st Nov[r] 1663. Witnesses, George
Conan there, and Andrew More in Oldmill
of Foveran.

3. Janet, buried 22d March 1660.

Besides Agnes Moir, b. 1668, Mrs. Pirie, Andrew
Moir I. of Oldmill had other children, see p. 6—a
son, James Moir, was bap. 6th Oct[r] 1659. Witnesses, Foveran
Ja[s] Scot in Meikle Haddo, and Alexander Houston Burial Regis-
in Balgerscho, and buried at Foveran July 5, 1660. ters.

Gilbert Moir in Pitmillan, described as tenant

and gentleman, with his wife and two children.—
Poll Book, vol. ii., pp. 150 and 153.

   1. Andrew, bap. 2d Jan[y] 1672. Witnesses,
      Andrew Moire, younger, and Andrewe
      Milne.

   2. Robert, bap. 10th May 1678. Witnesses,
      Ro[t] More, in Old Milne, and Ro[t] Milne, in
      Petmillan.

   3. Barbara, bap. 1st Jan[y] 1680. Witnesses,
      Andrew More and Thomas Grig.

   4. Isobel, bap. 27th Aug[t] 1683. Witnesses,
      Andrew Moir and Geo. Watson.

   5. Alexander, bap. 21st Aug[t] 1686. Witnesses,
      Alex[r] Johnston and Alex[r] Pirie.

   6. Janet, bap. 18th Nov[r] 1687. Witnesses,
      Andrew Moir, Alex[r] Pirie.

[1] Gilbert Moir, sometime in Haddo, Foveran
(another son, I think, of Andrew Moir I. of Oldmill, by his first wife)—

Foveran Reg.
of Baptisms.

   1. Elizabeth, bap. July 1675. Witnesses, James
      Scott and John Blair, both there.

   2. Anna, bap. 5th Jan[y] 1678. Witnesses, James
      Scot, Mr Alexander Johnstoune.

   3. Alexander, bap. 15th July 1680. Witnesses,
      Alex[r] Rose,[2] son to Mr. Jo[n] Rose,[3] and James

[1] It was not uncommon about this period to have two members
of a family baptized by the same Christian name, and in one
instance three of one family had all the same Christian names.—
Information from Rev. Walter Macleod of Edinburgh.

Forster's
Members of
Parliament,
p. 253. A Gilbert Moir was M.P. for Banff, 1646-7, and in 1648.

[2] Alexander Rose, son of the minister of Foveran, may have
been the ancestor of the Roses of Lethinty, see p. 13.—Scott's
" Fasti," &c.

[3] 1667, Minister of Foveran (D.D. 1684), died 1690, married
a dau. of the family of Udny of that ilk. His father, the Rev[d]

Scot in Haddo, and Mr. Alexʳ Burnet,
schoolmʳ at Foveran.

Gilbert Moir marries secondly—contract dated
9th Augᵗ 1681—Janet, dau. of the late Patrick
Forbes, sometime of Blackhall, of the ancient
family " of Pitsligo."—See contract, p. 42.

4. James, bap. 27th Septʳ 1682. Witnesses,
James Scot and James Moir.

5. William, ⎱ twins, bap. 1st June 1684. Wit-
6. Thomas, ⎰ nesses, Wm. Gordon and Wm.
Findlay, Thos. Forbes and Thos. Grig.

Robert Moir, in Overhill (probably a son of
Andrew Moir I., by his first wife), mᵈ.

He is described as tenant and gentleman there,
with his wife, 1695-6.—Poll Book, vol. ii., p. 151.

1. Agnes, bap. 16th May 1685. Witnesses,
Andʷ Moir and George Webster.

2. Isobel, bap. 12th Septʳ 1687. Witnesses,
Andʷ Moir and Robᵗ Temple.

3. Andrew, bap. 16th Augᵗ 1690. Witnesses,
Andʷ More and Andʷ Sutherland.

4. John, bap. 25 March 1693. Witnesses, John
Udny, John Scot.

5. Elspet, bap. 19th May 1694. Witnesses,
Alexʳ Pirie, Alexʳ Johnston.

The Foveran family of Moir seem to have had
daughters married to people named Catto, Connon,

Alexander Rose, Laird of Insch, in the Garioch, descended of
Kilravock, was Minister of Monymusk. Dr. John Rose of
Foveran succeeded to the paternal property of Insch. His brother,
Alexander Rose, was consecrated 1686 Bishop of Moray, and in
1688 Bishop of Edinburgh, while their uncle, Arthur Rose, was
Bishop of Argyll 1675, of Glasgow 1679; and who, in 1684,
became Archbishop of St. Andrews, and Primate of Scotland.

Johnston, Findlay, Webster, &c., and over two and a half centuries ago appear to have had a large connection in that district.

Foveran Reg. of Baptisms.

George Moir in Savock.

> 1. Barbara, bap. 20th July 1691. Witnesses, George Conan, Adam Mill.
> 2. William, bap. 27th June 1693.

Alexander Moir in Overhill, contracted 6th April, and m^d 1st May 1705 Janet Milne.

> 1. John, bap. 15th Novr 1705.
> 2. Issobel, bap. 21st July 1707.
> 3. Elspet, bap. 15th May 1709.
> 4. Barbara, bap. 21st July 1721.
> 5. Agnes, bap.   1723.
> 6. Jean, bap. 20th Decr 1726.

James Moir, in Newtyle, m^d 1st Jany 1704 Margaret Watson.

> 1. Janet, bap. 16th Feby 1707. Witnesses, Gilbert Moir in Pitmillan, and William Watson in Minnes (probably the paternal and maternal grandfathers).
> 2. Susanna, bap. 17th April 1709. Witnesses as before.

Of this prolific race of the Foveran Moirs, none known to be of this stock are now in the district. There is still the name in the parish. Mr. George Moir in Knockhall, whose progenitors came from Dyce, and the Moirs in Tarty, Logie-Buchan, who own part of the estate of Auchleuchries, in the parish of Cruden, whose descent I am not acquainted with.

A. J. M. G.

I.

ANDREW MOIR OF OVERHILL.

In the latter half of the seventeenth century, before there were so many outlets, as the opening up of the colonies, &c., half of the best farms in Aberdeenshire were in the hands of the sons and near connections of the gentry; and many of their descendants are still to be found occupying the same lands.

" Major opima ferat."
(Let the worthiest carry off the prize.)

ANDREW MOIR or MORE, sometime Laird of Overhill, the direct progenitor of the Moir-Byres family. B. in or about 1621. Was a wealthy Burgess of Aberdeen (admitted 11th Sept' 1688—see copy of Diploma, p. 45), and resided for many years at Oldmill,[1] in the parish of Foveran, in that county, where he died, at the age of 73, the 14th Dec' 1694, and was interred in the parish churchyard. For inscription on his tombstone see p. 16.

He was twice married, although I have been unable to ascertain the name of his first wife, and for an account of some of her children see pp. 6-9. His descendants preserve the following tradition, viz., " That previous to his second marriage he divided his property with the children of his first wife, in Foveran Registers and Tombstone.

---

[1] The house which this worthy built, lived, and died in, is still standing, and, architecturally speaking, it is superior to many of the Lairds' houses of that period.

order that he might not do them injustice, by be-
queathing too large a portion of his property at a
future period to children that might be born of the
proposed marriage." By his will (Aberdeen and
Banff wills were all nearly burned before 1721), made
1670-80, he left his wife and four children of the
second marriage 30,000 merks Scots—a large sum
in those days." Andrew Moir, who for a few
years after 1681 appears in the Foveran Register
of Baptisms, designed "of Overhill"—this had probably been the farm of that name, now on the
property of Blairythan, in the parish of Foveran—
married in 1670-72, for his second wife, Agnes
Montgomerie (b. 1650, died March 1730). For note
on family of Montgomerie, see p. 48, and tombstone
inscription, see p. 16.

Foveran
Registers.
ANDREW MOIR of Overhill and Oldmill, and
Agnes Montgomerie, had issue (Foveran Register
of Baptisms) five sons and three daughters—

1. ANDREW; of him again.
2. GILBERT, bap. 12th Feby 1675. Witnesses,
   Gilbert Moir in Haddo (see p. 8), and
   Gilbert Moir in Pitmillan (see p. 8). Was
   Muster-Master Depute in Scotland, and is so
   designed when admitted a Guild Brother of
   Aberdeen, 28th June 1716.
3. GEORGE, the Rev^d, M.A., bap. 12th May 1679.
   Witnesses, George Pirie, in Savock (probably
   a brother of Alexander Pirie, who m^d Agnes
   Moir, see p. 6), and George Conon, in
   Newtyle, was, according to Scott's "Fasti
   Ecclesiæ Scoticanæ," licensed 31st Octr 1705,
   called to Towie 21st Novr 1708, ordained

20th July 1709, translated to Cluny 3d
Octo^r 1717, and to Kintore 9th August
1727—(all in Aberdeenshire), and died there
9th April 1737. Mr. Moir was contracted
14th Decr 1718, and married 13th Jan^y
1719 to Jean Forbes, third daughter of Sir
William Forbes, IV. Baronet of Monymusk, in Aberdeenshire, by his wife, the
Lady Jean Keith, daughter of John I. Earl
of Kintore. Issue, two sons and two
daughters, viz. :—

1. William (b. 1726, d. 19th March 1794), the
Rev^d, M.A., licensed by Presbytery of
Ellon 4th Octr 1748, and presented that
date to Fyvie, in Aberdeenshire; ordained
27th April following (Scott's "Fasti,");
married 22d Octr 1776 Helen Constable
(who died at Aberdeen 26th Feby 1817,
aged 67), and had issue a son, George.
2. George, died young, unmarried.

1. Agnes, born 1723-9, married Alexander
Rose, eldest son of   Rose, Laird
of Lethinty, Aberdeenshire, and died in
1809 at the manse of Auchterless. Her
daughter, Jane Rose, b. 1754, married
1790 the Revd Alexander Rose,[1] minister of Auchterless, also in the county
of Aberdeen, and died in the town of
that name 22d Sept. 1820, leaving two

[1] Alexander Rose, A.M., translated from Drumoak, presented
by George III. to Auchterless 1774; died 7th Decr 1810, in his
84th year, and 47th ministry. M^d 1st. 14th Octr 1765 Sarah Gee
(d. 1789); 2dly, 5th Augt 1790 Jean Rose, p. 9.   Scott's "Fasti."

daughters—1. Agnes Rose, b. 1795, died
unm. in 1827; and 2. Jane Margaret
Rose, b. 1796, m. 1823 the Revd John
Johnston of Forgandenny, in the county of
Perth, and died 26th Septr 1832, leaving
two sons and two daughters, viz., 1. John
Robert Johnston, b. 1828, settled in New
Zealand, married 1850, and died 1862,
leaving two sons and four daughters;
2. Alexander Rose Johnston, b. 1832,
married 1866 Pauline, A. M., daughter of
Alexander Farquhar of Glenesk, Aberdeenshire. Issue, two sons and four
daughters — 1. Jane Taylor Johnston
(eldest dau. of Revd J. Johnston), b. 1825,
m. 1881 Andrew Paterson Reid of Tigh-
na-mara, Roseneath, co. Dumbarton; 2.
Agnes Rose Johnston (2d dau.), b. 1830,
married, 1869, Donald M. Macandrew,
merchant, of Leith, and now of Tor-
quay.

2. Jean Moir (second daughter of the Revd George
Moir and Jean Forbes), b. 1730, married
1751 James Jopp of Cotton (who died
1794), merchant in, and sometime Provost of, Aberdeen,[1] and died 1782. Issue
two daughters :—

    1. Jean Jopp, b. April 1755, married 24th
Jany 1799 Gavin Young of London,
merchant, and died 1836. (No issue.)

[1] James Jopp was Provost of Aberdeen from Michaelmas 1768
to 1770; again from 1772 to 1774; from 1776 to 1778; from
1780 to 1782, and in 1786.

2. Janet Jopp, married John Barnes of
East Finchley, Middlesex, and of the
Stock Exchange, and died 15th Nov^r
1848, leaving issue.

4. SAMUEL (son of Andrew Moir I. and Agnes Foveran
Registers.
Montgomery), baptized 21st June 1683.
Witnesses Robert Montgomery, see p. 49,
and Samuel Forbes (probably the same
person who afterwards succeeded to the
estate, and became II. Forbes Baronet of
Foveran).

5. JAMES, bap. 17th Augt 1689. Witnesses, James
Widowson and James Sutherland.

1. Margaret,¹ bap. Feby 18, 1677. Witnesses,
James Scott in Haddo, and Thomas Grig in
Linhead.

2. Marjory, bap. April 18, 1681. Witnesses, Ro-
bert Montgomery, see p. 48, in Groveshill.
Thomas Grig at ye Linhead, and Mr.
Daniel Taylor, Session-Clerk at Foveran.
Buried (at Foveran) 12th Augt 1681.

3. Isobel, bap. April 3, 1686. Witnesses, George Foveran
Registers.
Webster and Gilbert Moir.

Agnes Montgomerie, Tennant in Oldmill, is polled
as a gentlewoman. " Her proportione of the walua-
tione with the general poll is £1 : 9s. Andrew and
Margaret Mores, her children."—*Poll Book of Aberdeenshire*, vol. ii., p. 52, 1695-6.

¹ George Catto, tenant and gentleman in Monkshill, Foveran, Poll Book,
vol. ii. p. 166,
1695-6.
Margaret Moir, his wife, and Robert Catto, their son. She may
have been the eldest daughter of Andrew Moir I.—See above.
These Cattos were, I think, the progenitors of a respectable
family of Aberdeen merchants who were intermarried with the
Dingwalls of Rannieston, Lumsdens, &c.

Copy of Inscription on Andrew Moir's Tombstone,
Foveran Churchyard.

Here lyes under the hope of a blessed Ressurection,
Andrew More, Burgess of Abd., who departed this
life the 14 day of December 1694, and of his age 73
gomery
year—Also Agnes Mont spouse to Andrew Moir,
who died March 1730, aged 80 years—Likewise Andrew Moir, their eldest son, who died May 1733
aged 60 years—also Elizabeth Simpson, his Spouse,
who died 20 Sep. 1761, aged 86 years. Likewise Isobel
Moir, his daughter, spouse to John Meders, Burger
in Abdⁿ who died the . . . day of May 1777, aged 70.
Represented by the family of Moir-Byres of Tonley,
in the parish of Tough.

It will be observed that the surname is first spelt
More and afterwards Moir, on the tombstone.

1662. 7th Febʸ James Catto, in Upperhill (Overhill) of Foveran, brings an action against
Andrew Moir, at Oldmill, and Gilbert Clerk,
at the Kirk of Foveran.—(*Sheriff Court*
Records of Aberdeen.)

II.

ANDREW MOIR, born in or about 1673; died 2d May 1733. See tombstone inscription, former page. Settled at Cultercullen, in the parish of Foveran, and in 1728 has a renewal of the tack of Oldmill from Sir Alexander Forbes, Bart., of Foveran. He married 1699-1700, Elizabeth Simpson (b. 1675, died 20 Sept. 1761), daughter of Robert Simpson of Thornton, Aberdeenshire—see Simpson of Thornton, p. 51—and had issue four sons and four daughters, viz :—

1. ANDREW, his heir, b. 1703.
2. Robert, bap. 1st Novr 1712. Witnesses, Robert Moir in Greyshill, &c., alive (according to family papers) and resident at Little Mill of Esslemont, parish of Ellon, in 1746.

    Foveran Registers.

3. George, M.A., " Mr " " student in philosophy " (so designed in family papers), bap. by Mr. Alexander Gordon, minister, 12th Decr 1714. Witnesses, Robert Moir in Greyshill, and George Pirie in Savock, alive 1744.
4. Gilbert, bap. 2d May 1719, an eminent merchant of Aberdeen, and burgess of that town, acquired the property, and built the still existing mansion-house of Raeden, near Aberdeen; married in June 1745 Helen Shepherd (who died 8th Jany 1791), daughter of George Shepherd, merchant-burgess of Aberdeen, by his wife, Helen Thomson, of the family of "Thomson of Banchory," county Kincardine. Mr. More—so he and his

descendants spelt their surname—died 27th Nov[r] 1796, and is interred, along with many of his family and descendants, in the church-yard of St. Nicholas, Aberdeen, where there are several tombstones to the family. Issue, with children died young and un-married, two sons and two daughters, viz. :—

Burke's " Landed Gentry," art. " Innes of Raemoir."

1. George, II. of Raeden, merchant-burgess of Aberdeen, and Provost of that town from Michaelmas 1795 to 1797, and again from Michaelmas 1807 to 1809, married first Jane (who died 24th Feb[y] 1794), eldest daughter of Alex-ander Innes of Breda, co. Aberdeen, and of Cowie, co. Kincardine, advocate in and commissary clerk of Aberdeen, and had, with other issue, Gilbert More, of the Hon. E. I. Co.'s Civil Service, who died at Singapore, unmarried, 25th Aug[t] 1830. Provost More married, secondly, Harriet Beauvais of Aberdeen (who died 8th July 1855, aged 82), and by her had, with other issue, George More, Major in the Hon. H. E. I. Co.'s Service, married Jane Mitchell, daughter of James Mowat of Aberdeen, manufacturer, and had issue Charles More, chief engineer of the Thames Conservancy, and of 90 Sutherland Gardens, Maida Vale, Lon-don, W.

Provost More had by both his wives fourteen children.

2. Alexander, b. *circa* 1756. Sometime merchant in and Dean of Guild of Aberdeen, afterwards collector of customs at the port of that town; married Margaret (who died in Jany 1815, aged 42), fourth daughter of Alexander Innes of Breda and Cowie, and had issue. Mr. More died 30th April 1836.

1. Elizabeth, b. *circa* 1749, married Baillie Charles Farquharson of Aberdeen (who was in Decr 1809 accidentally killed by an explosion of gunpowder), and died April 1831.

2. Catherine, married in July 1792 James Thomson, advocate in Aberdeen, and cashier of the Aberdeen Banking Company, known by the *sobriquet* of "the Black Prince," and died at Aberdeen in July 1800, leaving issue.

Jean Moir (eldest daughter of Andrew Moir II. and Elizabeth Simpson of Thornton), bap. at Foveran 14th Mar. 1701. Witnesses, Mr. George Moir (the child's uncle, afterwards Minister of Towie, see p. 12), and William Annand, servitor to ye said Andrew Moir. Married (contract dated Augt 14) 2d Septr 1731, William Mitchell of Newburgh, Aberdeenshire, merchant, son of William Mitchell of Newburgh, merchant [1] (and elder

Foveran Register.

---

[1] This family of Mitchell have been connected with this district for at least 300 years, and are of the same stock as the Mitchells of Tillygreig, in the parish of Udny (whose arms are sable, a fesse wavy, between three mascles or); afterwards of Thainstone, in Kintore, and as Mitchell, of Colpna, now called Orrock, in Belhelvie, and were long connected with trading in grain and merchandise at the small shipping port of Newburgh.

brother of Alexander Mitchell, in Tillycorthie,[1] in
the adjoining parish of Udny, progenitor of the late
Alexander Mitchell, M.P., of Stow, in the county of
Edinburgh, and of the existing families of "Mitchell-
Innes" of Ayton Castle and Whitehall, in the shire
of Berwick, &c.

Jean Moir—Mrs. Mitchell—was interred in the
churchyard of Foveran 25th Jany 1792 (burial register
of the parish) ; issue three sons and two daughters,
viz. :—

1. William Mitchell, merchant-burgess of Aberdeen, acquired the lands of South Stocket,
near that town, bap. 13th Septr 1736, married
first, 1759, his relative, Elizabeth, daughter
and co-heir of John Middleton, younger of
Aberdeen, merchant, by Barbara Simpson,
of Concraig. (See Simpson of Thornton,
p. 53.) She died without issue. Mr. Mitchell married secondly, 1761-2, Mary (who
died 13th April 1824), daughter of William
Fordyce of Aquhorties, Baillie of Aberdeen
(of the eminent family of " Fordyce of Broad-
ford ;" another branch is Dingwall-Fordyce
of Brucklay), by his marriage in 1738 with

---

[1] Alexander Mitchell, in Tillycorthie, m. 1737 Isabel Temple.
One son was William Mitchell, in Haddo, p. 26 ; another, Alex-
ander Mitchell, m^d 1763 Elspet Simpson, a niece of George
Innes, I. of Stow, co. Edinburgh. Their eldest son, Thomas
Mitchell (was grandfather of the late Alexander Mitchell of Stow),
and another brother of last William Mitchell, J.P. and D.L., of
Parsons-Green, co. Edinburgh, assumed the additional surname
and arms of Innes, and was first of the Mitchell-Innes family of
Ayton and Whitehall, m^d 1810 Christian, dau. of Thomas Shairp
of Houston, co. Linlithgow, and had six sons and one daughter.—
See Burke's " Landed Gentry," art. "Mitchell-Innes of Ayton, &c.

Margaret, daughter of Walter Cochran of
Dumbreck, all in Aberdeenshire, see p. 79.
Mr. Mitchell died 10th May 1816, and was
interred in the churchyard of St. Nicholas,
Aberdeen. Issue, two sons and five daughters :—1st. William Mitchell, a Lieut. R.N.,
died unmar.; 2d. Walter Mitchell, Purser in
an East Indiaman man of war, under Admiral
Elliot, also died unmarried. 1st. Daughter,
Mary Mitchell, married William Paterson
of Aberdeen, advocate (no issue) ; 2d.
Elizabeth Mitchell, born in or about 1766,
married David Morrison, merchant-burgess
of Montrose, and had, with other issue,
James Martin Morrison, President of the
Manhattan Banking Company, New York,
married Jane Anne Macgowan, and has
issue; 3d. Margaret Mitchell, married James
Simpson of Aberdeen, merchant (no issue) ;
4th. Helen Mitchell, b. 1778, died young ;
5th. Elliot Mitchell, bap. Aug' 12, 1782— Register of
witnesses, Gilbert and George Moir, mer- St. Nicholas, Aberdeen.
chants (father and son), married James
Laurence of Aberdeen, manufacturer, and
has, with other issue, Walter Laurence,
Staff-Surgeon, R.N., married 1866 Hannah,
daughter of Francis Bennet, M.A., of Brigg,
co. Lincoln (without issue) ; and Elliot
Laurence, married the late Alexander
Ogston, J.P. of Ardoe, in the county of
Kincardine, representative of the ancient
family of " Ogston of that ilk," and had
issue.

2. Andrew Mitchell, b. 1737, died 13th May 1799,

settled about 1750 at Savock, in the parish of
Foveran, married 5th June 1759 Mrs. Margaret Cattanach (b. 1725, died 15th Feb^y
1815), granddaughter of Lumsden, Laird of
Corrachree,[1] parish of Logie-Coldstone (in
whose family she was brought up), cadet of
the old Aberdeenshire house of " Lumsden
of Cushnie." The date and initials of Mr.
and Mrs. Mitchell are on an old lintel slab
built into the present house of Savock,
thus—

17. A.M. M.C. 73.

Issue five sons and two daughters—*1st.*
William Mitchell, sometime in Pitgersie,
parish of Foveran, killed by a fall from his
horse in 1787, unmarried; *2d.* Andrew
Mitchell, who settled at Whiteness, in the
adjoining parish of Slains, m^d 1797, Isabel, dau. of Alexander Gray, in Knapleask,
in that parish, and their son is the present
Alexander Mitchell of Kincraig, a J.P. and
Commissioner of Supply for Aberdeenshire,
b. 1807, m^d, and has issue; *3d.* Alexander
Mitchell, b. 1769, settled at Fiddesbeg, in
the parish of Foveran, and his only son is
the present Andrew Mitchell of Logierieve,
in the parish of Udny, a property he bought
from the Ligertwoods, b. 1807, who is m^d,
and has issue; *4th.* John Mitchell, bap. Dec.

[1] For copy of a curious old letter from Mrs. Lumsden of Corrachree to her niece, Margaret Cattanach, see p. 66.

20, 1771, died young; 5*th.* Gilbert Mitchell, b. 1774, died 1844, II. of Savock, and who in 1813 took the additional farm of Haddo, also in the parish of Foveran, m^d in 1800. Margaret Bruce (b. 1782, died 1846), sister of the late James Bruce of Inverquhomery and Longside, a J.P. and Commissioner of Supply for Aberdeenshire. Of a family of seven sons and six daughters, none of the sons have left issue, excepting the eldest son, the late Andrew Mitchell, b. 1802, of Woodland Park, Tasmania, and Foveran House, Aberdeenshire, who m^d in 1858 Margaret, dau. of the late William Fasken of Fortrie, Banffshire; issue one son, Andrew William Mitchell, b. 1866, and two daughters—1st, Margaret Beatrice; 2d, Bertha Mary Bruce. Of the daughters of Gilbert Mitchell and Margaret Bruce, only three have issue, viz., Jane Mitchell, b. 1805, m^d 1839 the late James Pirie, Orchardton, parish of Udny, and Waterton, parish of Ellon—see note on family of Pirie, p. 7; issue, a son, James Mitchell Pirie (who m^d Elsie Harvey, and has a son, James Hunter Harvey Pirie), and two daughters, the second of whom, Jane Catherine Pirie, only is m^d (1878, as second wife), to John Leith-Ross of Arnage, Aberdeenshire (eldest son of John Leith-Ross, J.P. and D.L. of Arnage, afterwards referred to), and has issue, a dau., Jane Catherine Leith-Ross; 2d. Margaret Mitchell, b. at Savock 8th March 1809, m^d 1838 the late David Gill of Blair-

ythan and Savock [1] (only son of Patrick Gill
and Margaret Anderson, see Anderson of
Finshaugh, p. 58), a J.P. and Commissioner
of Supply for Aberdeenshire; issue, four
sons and one daughter, viz.—1. David Gill,
succ[d] 1878 to Blairythan, LL.D., F.R.A.S.,
F.R.S., J.P., &c., Astronomer Royal at
Cape of Good Hope since 1879, author of
several astronomical works, and a Knight
Commander of the Order of the Medjidie
(III. class), b. 1843, m[d] 1870 Isobel Sarah
(authoress of "Six Months in Ascension,
&c."), second dau. of John Black, of the
family of Black of Wateredgemuir," see p. 49 ;
2. Patrick Gilbert Gill of Monomeith, Victoria,
b. 1845 ; 3[d]. Andrew John Mitchell Gill,
who succ[d] 1878 to Savock, b. 1847, is a
Commissioner of Supply for the county, and
author of this Genealogy ; 4. James Bruce
Gill, b. 1849, of Runnymede, Victoria—1.

[1] This name, of Saxon or Scandinavian origin, is of great antiquity;
the barony of Gillsland, in Cumberland, was owned by a family
of the name before 1066. A branch of this stock from the north
of England is supposed to have settled in Perthshire (with which
county they were long connected) in the 14th century, where they
See "Genea- held the estates of Halton, Torsophy, &c. The family of Gill
logical Notes of Blairythan claim descent from John Gill of Halton, M.P. for
on Gill of
Blairythan, Perth, 1364-73, of which town either he or his son John Gill was
&c."—(Scott Provost. Their direct ancestor, Alexander Gill, b. about 1550,
& Ferguson,
Edinburgh.) dead 1618, settled at Auchlyne, in Buchan, Aberdeenshire, in
which he was succeeded by his son Robert. With this district
his descendants have since been connected. Arms of Gill of
Blairythan—Lyon Register—Fusily argent and vert on a chief
gules, three martlets of the first. Crest—a demi-eagle rising
proper. Mottos—"Sursum Prorsusque" (Upward and Onward),
and below shield, "In te Domine spes nostra" (In thee, O Lord,
is our trust).

Margaret Gill, m^d 17th Jany 1882 Revd Henry
Powell (M.A., Clare, Cambridge), Rector and
Patron of Stanningfield, Suffolk; issue, a son,
Henry Mitchell Powell, b. 21st May 1883;
3*d*. Barbara Mitchell (youngest daughter
of Gilbert Mitchell and Margaret Bruce),
m^d 1845 her cousin, John Ruxton (son of
Charles Ruxton and Anne Ligertwood),
M.A., M.D., and L.R.C.S., and has a large
family, of which the eldest son, John Ruxton,
M.D., late of the 17th Leicestershire Reg^t,
A.M.D., now of Blackpool, Lancashire,
m^d 1884 his cousin-german, Jane Birnie,
eldest dau. of Thomas Ruxton of Craigton,
advocate in Aberdeen.

1. Jean Mitchell (eldest dau. of Andrew Mitchell and Mrs. Margaret Cattanach),
   m^d 1783 John Ligertwood (son of Thomas
   Ligertwood, in Cairnhill, Ellon, and Margaret Gordon, of the family of Hallhead,
   afterwards referred to), in Overhill and
   Pitscaff, Foveran, and had a large family
   (one dau., Anne Ligertwood, m^d Charles
   Ruxton, see above); their eldest grandson
   is John Ligertwood, J.P., of Bucksburn,
   advocate in and sheriff and commissary
   clerk of Aberdeen ; m^d, and has issue.

2. Margaret Mitchell, m^d 1798 her cousin-
   german, Alexander Mitchell, in Haddo,
   son of William Mitchell there, and had
   issue.

3. Alexander Mitchell, bap. 24th Nov. 1740, (must
   have died young).

D

1. Elizabeth Mitchell (eldest dau. of William
   Mitchell and Mrs. Jean Moir), b. 1733, m^d
   1756 her cousin-german, William Mitchell,
   in Haddo, Foveran, son of Alexander
   Mitchell of Tillycorthie—see p. 20—and
   had with other issue Alexander Mitchell, II.
   of Haddo; m^d his cousin, as above.
2. Jean Mitchell, b. 1735, m^d . . Shepherd;
   no issue.

2. Agnes Moir (second dau. of Andrew Moir II. and
   Elizabeth Simpson of Thornton), bap. 5th Feb^y
   1705; witnesses, Robert Pittendreigh, younger,
   and George Duff, in Oldmill, married—contract
   dated 16th Nov^r) Decr 10, 1732. George Gray,
   merchant in Boghouse, parish of Tarves, son of
   George Gray in Haddo, Foveran.
3. Isobel Moir (third dau. of Andrew Moir II.),
   bap. 21st April 1707; witnesses, Robert Simpson of Thorntoune, the child's grandfather, and
   George Duff, in Oldmill; married John Meders,
   burgess of Aberdeen, and died in 1777.
4. Elizabeth Moir (fourth dau. of Andrew Moir II.),
   bap. 6th Augt 1709; witnesses, Mr. George Moir,
   minister of Towie, the child's uncle, and Robert
   Simpson of Thornton; married—contract dated
   26th May 1744. James Gray, sometime in
   Overhill, and afterwards in Mains of Foveran,
   another son of George Gray in Haddo; issue
   at least one son and one daughter.

   1. George Gray, bap. 20th April 1745.
      See next page.

   1. Elizabeth Gray, married James Milne of

Rosehearty, merchant,[1] and had a son, George Milne, b. 1777 ; married 1821 Margaret, daughter of William Milne of the same place (she died 1855), and had with other issue George Milne of Westwood, banker in Aberdeen, b. 1826, married 1862 Williamina, third daughter of the late John Panton, in Knockiemill, Turriff, Aberdeenshire, and has issue.

The other children of George Milne of Rosehearty and Margaret Milne were, besides—

1. George, of Westwood, banker, see above.
2. James, late Banker of Elgin, and now of Helensburgh, born 1828, married 1869 Elizabeth, daughter of John Sidney Wardlaw, W.S., of Edinburgh, and has issue.
3. William, died young.
1. Isabella, married 1841 Alexander Robertson, Town-Clerk of, and Solicitor in Peterhead, Aberdeenshire, and has issue.
2. Elizabeth, married the Rev[d] Charles Wedderburn of Edinburgh, and has issue.

James Gray, in Overhill, had also by his wife, Elizabeth Moir, a son, George Gray, bap. 20th April 1745. Witnesses, George Gray, in Meikle Haddo (the child's grandfather), and William Mitchell, at Bridgefoot (the child's uncle by marriage). Fovernn Register.

---

[1] Of five sons and two daughters of James Milne and Elizabeth Gray, all died unmarried, or without leaving issue, excepting the third son, George Milne, b. 1777. See above.

III.

ANDREW MOIR, the Rev[d], M.A. (eldest son of II. Andrew Moir of Oldmill and Elizabeth Simpson of Thornton), bap. in the kirk of Foveran 13th Aug[t] 1703. Witnesses, Andrew Moir, in Old Aberdeen, and Andrew Jaffray, in Cultercullen. Was, according to Scott's " Fasti," licensed 9th Aug[t] 1727, ordained and placed at Towie 11th Sept[r] 1728, translated to Methlick 31st May 1739, and from there to Ellon, all in Aberdeenshire, 24th April 1745, of which place he died minister 19th March 1774, and is interred with his wife and several members of his family in the churchyard there. On outside of church of Ellon, there is a tablet to his memory. Mr. Moir married 7th Sept[r] 1737 Jane (who died in Oct[r] 1789, aged 74), daughter of the Rev[d] William Forbes of Tarves (a younger son of Sir John Forbes of Waterton, Knight—see that family, p. 54—by his wife, Jean Gordon, sister of George, I. Earl of Aberdeen), by Janet, his wife, daughter of Prof. James Gregory, inventor of the Reflecting Telescope—see families of Gregory and Anderson, pp. 63 and 56,—issue, three sons and three daughters, viz. :—

1. GEORGE, the Rev[d], his heir.
2. William, born 2d Nov[r] 1750, who died in London unmarried.
3. Andrew, born 28th April 1753.

Of the daughters, Janet (the second), born 10th Oct[r] 1743, died unmarried, and Jane (the third), born 8th Nov[r] 1745, also died unmarried 16th Sept[r] 1816.

Elizabeth Moir (eldest daughter of the Rev. Andrew Moir and Jane Forbes), born 6th Novr 1739, married Robert Garden, sometime designed of Grange and Clerkhill, both in Aberdeenshire, Baron Baillie of Peterhead, and advocate in Aberdeen (admitted in June 1784). The register of Peterhead gives the following children :—

1. James Garden, }
2. Alexander, } twins, born 4th March, and bap. 6th, 1770. Witnesses, the Revd George Moir (uncle of the children), and Capt Harry Gilchrist, in Fraserburgh.
3. Francis Garden, bap. 23d June 1771. Witnesses, Revd George Moir and Alexander Reid, in Blackhouse.
4. Robert Garden, bap. June 5, 1763. Witnesses, James Arbuthnot and Charles Smith, merchants there.
5. Andrew Garden, bap. 13th Decr 1765. Witnesses, Capt John Thomson, shipmaster, and Dr. Thomas Gordon of Clerkhill.

1. Janet Garden, born Novr 28, and bap. 30th, 1767. Witnesses, Revd George Moir and Dr. Thomas Gordon of Clerkhill. Married Major Robertson, and had four daughters :— *1st.* Elizabeth Robertson, married Dr. George Fyfe ; *2d.* Jessie Robertson, married Capt F. E. Loch, R.N., fourth son of George Loch of Drylaw, in the county of Edinburgh, and has issue ; *3d.* Catherine Robertson, married Adam Gibb Ellis of Edinburgh, W.S. (no issue) ; *4th.* Rachel Robertson, married George Brodie, advocate in Edin-

burgh, and Historiographer-General for Scotland.

2. Mary Garden, bap. 27th Decr 1768. Witnesses, Revd George Moir, and George Gordon of Sheelagreen (relative of Mrs. George Moir's, see sequel).

3. Jean Garden, bap. 17th Augt 1764. Witnesses, George Gordon of Sheelagreen, and Dr. Thomas Gordon of Clerkhill.

Of the sons of Elizabeth Moir and Robert Garden, one was a Colonel in the Army, and died unmarried. Another son, George Garden (not in above list), settled as a merchant at Montreal, married his relative, Euphemia, daughter of William Forbes of Echt, Aberdeenshire—(see family of Forbes of Waterton, p. 55)—and had at least two sons—viz., Robert Garden of London, married (no issue), and William Garden, also of London, married, and has issue.

Of the other daughters of Elizabeth Moir and Robert Garden, one became Mrs. Garland of Cairnton, near Fordoun, and had issue; another, wife of Lieut. Forsyth, R.N., of Harthill, Aberdeenshire, and had issue; another married Andrew Nicol of Aberdeen, of the same family as Nicol of Ballogie, in Aberdeenshire, and had issue; and another became Mrs. Greig, and had issue; her husband was a farmer in Forfarshire.

IV.

The Revd GEORGE MOIR, M.A., born at Ellon 5th April 1741, took his degree of M.D. at Marischal College, Aberdeen; diploma dated 1765; was, according to Scott's "Fasti," licensed 26th April, presented by George III., 6th May 1765, to Peterhead, and ordained 11th August following. Of this much respected gentleman, who was for the long period of fifty-five years minister of Peterhead, it is told that he had at the same place, at different times, "three churches, three manses, and thrice an augmentation of his living." Dr. Moir had a sexton who lived in the Kirkton of Peterhead named Mutch, and he was fond of saying, "that there is Mutch in the Kirkton, but Moir (often pronounced *More*) in the manse." He wrote "The Statistical Account of the Parish of Peterhead," which is very valuable.

Dr. Moir, who died 18th March 1818, and is interred at Peterhead, married, 7th August 1766, Martha, third daughter of Patrick Byres I. of Tonley —(see that family [1])—and commenced the connection between the Moirs and Byres, which has resulted in their being merged into one family.

Mrs. Moir died in Novr 1816, aged 77, and was buried beside her husband. Issue, eight sons and two daughters, viz.[2] :—

    1. Andrew, bap. June 12, 1767. Witnesses, Robert Garden, baillie (the child's uncle by _{Register of} marriage), and Dr. Thomas Gordon of Clerk- _{Peterhead.}

[1] Copy letter from Earl Marischall, see p. 66.
[2] There are fine portraits of this couple at Tonley, painted by their son, John Moir.

hill. An officer in the army, died in India, unmarried.

2. Patrick, or Peter (so called in Register), bap. July 5, 1769. Witnesses, Peter Buyers of Tonley, and George Gordon of Sheelagreen. Was Secretary to Lord Minto, Governor-General of India, whom he accompanied to Bengal in 1807, and was appointed Commissioner of the Court of Requests at Calcutta in the same year; a trust which he discharged with integrity, assiduity, and ability to the time of his decease, which occurred there 5th Feb[y] 1810. For inscription on his tombstone, erected by his friend and patron, Lord Minto, see p. 67.[1]

Register of Peterhead. 3. JAMES, bap. 14th Nov[r] 1770. Witnesses, George Gorden, Sheelagreen, and Bailie Robert Garden of Clerkhill. Of him again, see p. 36.

4. Robert, bap. 24th March 1772. Witnesses, Mr. David Wilson, surgeon, and George Gordon of Sheelagreen. Died unmarried.

5. John, born in or about 1775, well known in the north-east of Scotland as an artist, and in not a few of the country houses there are his portraits to be seen. He acquired the small property of St. Catherine's, near Peterhead, where he often resided, and died 28th Feb[y] 1859, and was interred beside his parents in Peterhead Churchyard. Mr. Moir married, in 1800, his cousin-german Catherine, eldest daughter and co-heir of Captain John Byres,

[1] There is a fine portrait, by Raeburn, of this gentleman in the possession of his nephew Mr. Moir-Crane.

R.E.—(See Byres of Tonley.) Issue, four sons and three daughters, viz. :—

    1. George, born at Ambleside, Westmoreland, where he died an infant.

    2. Patrick Moir-Byres, IV. of Tonley—see that family.

    3. James Gregory Moir-Byres, V. of Tonley, see that family.

    4. George Moir-Byres, VI. and now of Tonley, see that family.

    1. Isabella, died unmarried.

    2. Catherine, married first John-Foster Fraser; issue, two sons, viz., John Fraser and George Patrick Fraser; and secondly, William Findlay.

    3. Stuart, married 3d April 1849 James Balvaird-Bathgate Junor, and has one son, George Moir Junor, born 2d Jany 1850.

6. William, sometime a writer in Edinburgh, went to Trinidad, and died there unmarried 31st Augt 1802.

7. Forbes, died young.

8. Andrew, of Quebec, merchant, died there unmarried in 1832.

1. Janet Moir (eldest daughter of the Revd George Moir and Martha Byres), married first Christopher Norton[1] of Penkridge and Congrave, in the county of Stafford, to whom she had one son and two daughters, viz. :—

    1. James Christopher Norton, a Lieut. in the Hon. E. I. Company, died in India, unmarried.

---

[1] Son of Christopher Norton of Penkridge, &c.

E

1. Louisa Latifer Norton, who became the
   first wife of Alexander Copland,
   advocate, Aberdeen, son of Professor Patrick Copland of the same
   place, and had issue—
2. Martha Norton, died unmarried.

Janet Moir, married, secondly, Captain John
Davidson of Gottenburgh, to whom she had two
sons, viz. :—

1. George Moir Davidson, minister of Watten, in
   Caithness, married Isabella, daughter of the
   Rev[d] William Grant of Sandy, in the island
   of Orkney. Issue six sons and two
   daughters, viz.[1] :—
   1. George William Davidson, born 1836,
      Professor of Anatomy in the Veterinary
      College, Edinburgh ; died unmarried.
   2. John Kerr Davidson, D[r] of Blackburn, Lan-
      cashire, married Mary, daughter of Cap-
      tain Woodruffe, R.N., and had issue.

2. Patrick Moir Davidson, some time an
   officer East India Mercantile Service,
   married Sophia, daughter of Captain

---

[1] The Rev[d] G. M. Davidson of Watten and Isabella Grant—

3. Patrick Moir Davidson, D[r] of Congleton, b. 3d Feb[y]
   1844, m[d] first, Anna Phipps, dau. of William Boileau
   of Dublin, merchant, and secondly, Emily Stainforth.
4. James Andrew Davidson, ⎫ Both deceased.
5. Robert Davidson, ⎭
6. David Charles Davidson, Surgeon, Indian Army, married
   Edith F. Meynell, second dau. of Major-General
   Clarke, formerly Commissioner of Oudh.

1. Jessie Moir Davidson, died 1844.
2. Isabella Davidson.

Charles White, Commissioner at Antigua, West Indies. Issue, with a son, Patrick Howard White, died in infancy. One daughter, Sophia Davidson, married first, 26th Augt 1856, George Ranken, Lieut.-Col. 69th Bengal N.I., and had (with other issue, died young)—*1st.* George Patrick Ranken, born 13th Octr 1859, Lieut. 6th Bengal N.I. ; *2d.* Jessie Georgina Ranken, married 1876 her cousin, John Claude White, C.E., and has issue. Sophia Davidson (Mrs. Ranken) married, secondly, 1876, Dr William Michael MacGrath, of Bayswater, and has a son, Michael Reginald MacGrath.

2. Jane Moir (second daughter of Revd George Moir), became first wife of the Revd William Donald of Peterhead. (No issue.)

V.

JAMES MOIR, M.D. (third son of the Rev⁴ George
Moir and Martha Byres of Tonley, see p. 32), bap.
at Peterhead 14th Nov' 1770, was sometime of
Johnston, Rubislaw, near Aberdeen, and afterwards
of Braehead, near Old Aberdeen. Dr. Moir, who
was one of the leading physicians of his day in
Aberdeen—see next page—died there in Nov'
1861, and was interred in St. Nicholas Churchyard,
in the vault of his maternal ancestors, the Donaldsons of Auchmull.[1] He married in 1802 his cousin-
german Janet (who died 1818, and was also interred
in the Donaldson vault), youngest daughter and co-
heir of Cap' John Byres, R.E., by his wife, Isobel
Donaldson of Auchmull.—See families of Byres
and Donaldson.

1. James, died young, b. 1817, d. 1826.
2. Patrick, his heir.
1. Janet (Jessie), of Bon Accord St., Aberdeen ;
     died unmarried 1870.

THE LATE DR. JAMES MOIR.

From " Aberdeen Journal," November 1861.

We observed the name of this old and respected citizen in our
obituary of the bye-past week, and cannot let it pass without some
slight notice of the event.

---

[1] Inscription on tombstone—" Under this stone, in the place of
sepulture appropriated during 200 years for her maternal ancestors
of the name of Donaldson, the last of Auchmull, are deposited the
remains of Janet, wife to Dr. Moir, Physician in Aberdeen, who
died in the 17th June 1818, æt. 37. Also of their son James, who
died in April 1826, aged 9 years ; and of the above Dr. Moir,
who departed this life 4th Nov' 1861, aged 91." &c.

Dr. Moir was born at Peterhead in 1770, being the son of the minister of the parish ; and having received the early portion of his education partly there, and partly at the Academy of Mary-culter, under the charge of Dr. Glennie, he entered the classes at Marischal College, and passed through the usual course of study at the University. Being destined for the medical profession, he became a pupil of the late Dr. George French, who was Professor of Chemistry ; and while thus engaged, he, along with a few fellow-students, among whom was the late Sir James M'Gregor, for the sake of mutual improvement, met together, and instituted the Medico-Chirurgical Society on the 15th of December 1789. He subsequently went to Edinburgh, and completed his medical educa-cation under the superintendence of his relative, Dr. James Gregory, Professor of Medicine in the University, and graduated there about the year 1792. He was soon after attached as surgeon to the Hopetoun Fencibles, and continued with this corps till it was dis-embodied in 1798. After this Dr. Moir settled permanently in Aberdeen as a medical practitioner. He was elected one of the medical officers of the Royal Infirmary in 1808, and resigned this ap-pointment in 1814. He was also appointed surgeon to the Aberdeen Bridewell after its erection ; and, besides conducting an extensive private practice, he took an active interest in the management and prosperity of the various public charities and institutions of the city. Though originally of a strong constitution, he began to feel the infirmities of age approaching, and, after a long and laborious medical career, he finally retired from the practice of his profession in 1843, and from this time lived in the quietness of private life at his cottage of Brachead, near Balgownie, enjoying the respect and affection of his friends and neighbours. He continued to possess remarkably good health, and was seldom confined to his bed till within a few days of his death, which took place, without a struggle, on the 4th November 1861—thus wanting only six days to complete his ninety-first year. His funeral was conducted on Monday, the 11th November, from the hall of the Medico-Chirur-gical Society in King Street—the remains being preceded by the President and Members of the Society walking in procession—to the Churchyard of St. Nicholas, out of respect to his memory. Any lengthened eulogium on the deceased would be out of place. His habits were domestic and retiring, and he avoided public notice and display. As a practitioner, he was much esteemed for his accurate and extensive knowledge, and the kindness and condescension he showed in his intercourse with his brethren. The same qualities were no less felt in his intercourse with his patients; though sometimes he might startle by the abruptness of his manner, his wonted urbanity soon reconciled them to him, and they came to regard him with much confidence and affection. In fact, under a certain roughness of exterior there lay concealed much tenderness and feeling, too often called forth during those scenes of affliction and distress which medical men are so frequently obliged to witness in the course of their professional duties. To the poor he gave largely of his time and skill, without the least expectation of being remunerated. He was a sincere Christian, and kind and benevolent to all.

VI.

PATRICK MOIR, present head and representative of this branch of the Moir family. Born 1813. Assumed the additional surname of Crane,[1] and is now of Crowcroft, Levenshulme, Lancashire. Married 1838 Maria, eldest daughter of John White, merchant, of Quebec—see family of White, p. 68. Issue seven sons and three daughters.

1. George, now of Stoneywood, Victoria Park, Manchester. Born 23d April 1839. Married 11th Aug[t] 1866 Sophia Matilda, eldest daughter of Andrew Hume Bulteel, of Her Majesty's Customs, Liverpool—see family of Bulteel, p. 68. Issue, five sons and two daughters, viz. :—

   1. Patrick, born 10th Oct[r] 1869.
   2. George Bulteel, born 29th Sept[r] 1870.
   3. Edward Byres, born 30th June 1873.
   4. Douglas, born 31st Jan[y] 1875.
   5. James Sandilands, born 28th July 1881.
   1. Sophie.
   2. Mabel.

2. James, born 1st July 1842, merchant, of Albany, U.S., married 20th April 1870, Alice Catherine, daughter of Edward Andrews, M.D., of Titchfield, Hants. Issue (with a son, Byres, and two daughters, Alice-

[1] The sons of Mr. Moir-Crane drop the surname of Crane.

Maud and Mary Helen, died young), two
sons and two daughters :—

   1. James Douglas, b. 29th Augt 1871.
   2. Gordon, b. 27th Octr 1877.
   1. Alice-Hilda.   2. Dorothea.

3. Douglas, M.D., of Manchester, born 15th June
   1844, married 6th Decr 1876 Mary Flo-
   rence, daughter of Edward Wood of Manchester, merchant. Issue two sons and one
   daughter, viz. :—

   1. Edward, born 14th Jany 1878.
   2. Douglas, born 1st Septr 1883.
   1. Marjory Douglas.

4. John, born 27th July 1848, married 30th June
   1880 Esther Anne Mallaber, daughter of
   William Lowndes-Yates of Congleton,
   Cheshire. Issue two sons :—

   1. Howard Lowndes, b. 7th Augt 1881.
   2. John Lowndes, b. 20th Decr 1882.

5. Patrick, born 22d March 1850, married 16th
   April 1879 Anne, daughter of Charles Smith
   Ross and Euphemia Buchan Cruden, both
   of Aberdeenshire.
6. Byres, M.B., of Leinster Square, Bayswater,
   London. Born 5th April 1853.
7. Richard, born 27th Jany 1855.
1. Jessie Caroline, married 23d June 1870 John
   Hill of Manchester, merchant. Issue four
   sons and two daughters, viz. :—

   1. Harold James, born 6th Septr 1874.
   2. Claude John Gomes, born 3d July
    1877.

       3. Cyril Patrick, born 28th June 1879.
       4. Francis Joseph, born 15th Novr 1880,
          died July 20th 1881.
       1. Florence Maria White.
       2. Evelyn Rebecca, died young.

2. Caroline, married 20th June 1872 James
   Hutchison of Liverpool, merchant, and has
   issue—
       1. Robert Leonard, b. 4th Novr 1876.
       2. Allan Moir, b. 20th March 1878.
       1. Caroline Maria.
       2. Kathleen Gilmour.
       3. Margaret Constance.

3. Maria.

CONTRACT of MARRIAGE, GILBERT MOIR and JANET FORBES, 1681.

Att Linnheid, the nynt day of August J^mvi^c four-scoir ane yeires, it is appoyntit, contractit, and agriet vpon betwixt Gilbert Moir, in Haddo off Foveran, on the ane pairt, and Janet Forbes, laufull daughter to vmquhill Patrick Forbes, see p. 9, sumtyme off Black-hall,[1] on the vther pairt, in manner, forme, and to the effect efterspecifeit : That is to say, the said Gilbert Moir and Janet Forbes obleidges thame to solemnise and accomplish the holie band of matrimonie, ilk ane of thame tuo with the vther, in face of holie kirk, be the wordis of the present tyme, and that with all convenient dilligence efter the subscryveing of thir presents, and thereafter to love, cherish, and inter-taine ilk ane of thame the vther as Christiane mairied personis of their degrie and qualitie, swa long as it shall pleas God that they two lives togidder : In contemplatione of the quhilk marriage, and for the better proceiding therintill, the said

---

[1] Forbes of Blackhall was a cadet of the old family of Pitsligo, thus—Patrick Forbes of Blackhall, a grandson of Alexander Forbes VI. of Pitsligo, called " the Red Laird," by Beatrix, dau. of the Lord Saltoun) m^d . . . issue :—

    1. John, M.D., the Rev^d (degree 1668), minister, first of Coldstone, translated to Kincardine-O'Neil 1680. Witness to above contract 1681.—(Scot's Fasti, p. 534, part vi.)

    2. Alexander, in Benwalls, also a witness, probably another brother.

    1. Janet, m^d 1681 Gilbert Moir.

    2. Isobel, m^d 16th Feby 1664 the Revd John Mair of Tough (1663).—Scot's Fasti, ibid., p. 566, and had issue.

Janet Forbes hes desponit and heirby disponis to
the said Gilbert Moir, hir futur husband, all and
sundrie guidis, geir, insight plinishing, or vtheris
quhatsomever pertening to hir and now in hir
possessioune. And sicklyke hes made and constitute,
and be thir presentis makis and constituts the said
Gilbert Moir, his airis, executouris, or assignayes,
hir laufull cessioneris and assignayes in and to the
saidis guidis, geir, insight plinisheing, or vthers
quhatsomever pertening to hir and now in hir
possessioune. And sicklyke in and to all and sundrie
debts and soumes of money, guidis, or geir addebtit
and resting oweing to hir, be quhatsumever persone
or personis, either vpone band, obligatioune, contract,
dispositione, tiket, promise, letterwill, testament,
legacie, provisione, or otherwayes quhatsumever;
And surrogats and substitutis the said Gilbert Moir,
hir said futur husband, and his forsaidis, in hir full
vice and place of the premissis, with full power to him
and his above writtine to call and persew for pay·
ment of the saidis debtis, to intromitt with, uplift, and re-
ceave the said guidis, geir, insight and plinisheing,
to sell vs and dispon thairupon at his pleasour, dis-
penseing with the generalitie heirof, and admitting
and declairing the samen to be als valid and sufficient in all respects, as if everie particullar of the
saidis guidis, geir, insight plinisheing, debts, soumes
of money, and uthers above specifeit wer heirin
insert, ingrossit, disponit, and assignit per expres-
sume: In consideratione quhairof, and for the said
Jannet Forbes hir lyfrent provisione, the said
Gilbert Moir bindis and obleidges him, his airis,
executouris, and successouris, to wair, bestow, and

imploy the soume of ane thousand merkis Scotis
money upon land, band, merchandice, husbandrie,
guidis, geir, or vther penieworthis, wher best imploy-
ment may be hade for the tyme, and to sufficientlie
secur and provyd the forsaid soume of ane thousand
merks money forsaid to himself and the said Janet
Forbes, his said futur spous, the langest liver of
thame two in lyfrent, and to the bairnis to be
procreat betwixt thame in fie, quhilks failzieing, to
the said Gilbert Moir, his owne neirest airis, executouris, or assignayes quhatsumever. With this provisione alwayes, that the saidis guidis, geir, debtis,
and soumes of money now perteining to the said
Janet Forbes, and disponit and assigneit be hir in
maner forsaid, shalbe a pairt of the forsaid soume
of ane thousand merkis, quhairinto shoe is provydit
in lyfrent and hir bairnes in fie, in maner above
mentionit: And both pairties ar content and con-
sents thir presentis be insert and registrat in the
bookis of counsill and sessione, sheref or commissar
bookis of Aberdein, ther to remaine *ad futuram
rej memoriam*, that letteris and executoriallis neces-
sar in forme as effeiris may be direct thairon, and
constituts   ,
their procuratouris, &c.—In witness quhairof, thir
presents (writtine be James Cuming, notar publict)
ar subscryveit with their handis, day, yeir, and place
forsaid, befoir thir witnessis, Alexander Forbes, in
Benvallis, Maister Johne Forbes, minister at Cold-
stane, and the said James Cuming.

(Signed)   GILBERT MOIR.
            J. F.

(Signed)   A. Forbes, *witnes.*
        John fforbes, *witnes.*
        J. Cuming, *witnes.*

1688. Burgess' Diploma in favour of Andrew Moir, at Old Mill of Foveran, see p. 11.

At Aberdeen, the eleventh day of the month of September 1688, in presence of the provest, baillies, dean of gild, treasurer, and several of the councillors of the said burgh ; on which day Andrew Moir, at the Old Mill of Foveran, was received and admitted as a free burgess and gild brother of the aforesaid burgh of Aberdeen, for the composition of thirty pounds money of this kingdom, paid to the dean of gild, with ten pounds for the gild wine, for good considerations moving them ; five shillings being also paid to the provest in a white purse, as the manner is, and the usual oath being given by the said burgess.

Extracted from the books of the Council of the said burgh by me,

H^w Robertson.

(*Translated from the original in Latin*).

ARMORIAL BEARINGS of the Family of
MOIR or MORE in Scotland, from the " Lyon
Register."

I. Doctor William Moir, of Scotstoune, bears
argent three negroes' heads coupé, proper, with a
ribband or scarf about ye brow knit behind, of
the first ; above ye shield ane helmet befitting his
degree, mantled gules, doubled, argent. Next is
placed on ane torse for his crest a mort head upon
two leg bones saltyre ways, proper. The motto in
the escroll—" Non sibi sed cunctis."—(Not for self,
but for all.)

Registered 1672-78.

II. John Moir, of Stoneywood, argent three
mouritannian heads, couped, and distilling gutt de
sang, proper. Crest, a mouritannian head couped as
ye former. Motto—" Major opima ferat."—(Let
the worthiest carry off the prize).

Same date.

III. James Moir, of Invernethie, Esquire, pater-
nally descended from the family of Stoneywood,
argent three Moor's heads couped, each wreathed
with laurel, and distilling three drops of blood, all
proper; in chief, a dexter hand pointing with the
fore-finger towards the base of the last, crest an eye
proper. Motto—" Deus dedit." — (God gave).
Matriculated 27th Jany 1792.

1792.

IV. Master William More, of Hilton, Advocate,
bears or, three men's heads couped, distilling drops
of blood proper, wreathed about with bay leaves,

1672-78.

vert. Crest, a dexter arm issuing from the shoulder out of a cloud, and holding a branch of laurel, slipped, all proper. Motto—" Virtute non aliter."—(By virtue, not otherwise.)

V. Thomas Moir, of Otterburne, whose grand-father was a second son of ye familie of Abergeldie, argent three Negroes' heads couped, proper, within a bordure, counter indented, sable, and ar. Crest, a Same date. negroe's head, as the former. Motto—" Medio-criter."—(With moderation).

FAMILY OF MONTGOMERY.

"Gardez bien "—(Guard well).

Simple arms, azure, three fleurs de lis or.

The first of this name in Scotland was Robert de Montgomery, who received a grant of the lands of Eglisham, in Renfrewshire, 1160-1175, died about 1177. From him comes the noble family of Montgomery, Earls of Eglintoun, and many others.

Of Agnes Montgomerie or Montgomery, wife of Andrew Moir, I. of Oldmill, born 1650, died March 1730, see p. 12, I have been able to find out very little about. All I presently know of her family is from a scrap of paper, amongst the family papers of Mr. George Moir of Stoneywood, near Manchester, addressed to Provost More,—*i.e.*, George More of Raeden, who was Provost of Aberdeen 1795-97, and again from 1807-9, see p. 18,—in the handwriting, I think, of his cousin, the late Dr. James Moir, of Aberdeen, viz., "Hay of Renneston [1] (a property in Logie-Buchan, Aberdeenshire, now held by the Dingwall family), went to Berwickshire or Northumberland (more probably Ayrshire) and married a Miss Montgomerie. Her sister, Agnes Montgomerie, came with her, and married Oldmill (that is, Andrew Moir). *N.B.*, that was the last Rennieston's father. I believe Rob[t] Simpson of Thornton's wife (see p. 50) was some connection of the Montgomeries, for he, Rob[t] Simpson, got acquainted with his wife by the connection of the Oldmill people." The matter within brackets is added.—No doubt Agnes Montgomerie's or Moir's people, had originally come from the south country, as above stated, but there were families of the surname located in Foveran and the neighbourhood over two centuries ago.

Probably written 1795 to 1809.

1661. Dec[r] 2. John Montgomerie in Tillycorthie, parish of Udny— (Sheriff Court Records of Aberdeen.)

Reg. of B[p]. of Foveran Parish.

1680. April 28. Robert Montgomerie in Groveshill (Greyshill probably ; a farm in Foveran), is a witness to the baptism

---

[1] Alexander Hay of Rannieston, died before 16th Nov[r] 1721, when his will is recorded. He had probably been a son of Hay of Rannieston, by Miss Montgomery, the sister of Agnes Montgomery, wife of Andrew Moir, I. of Oldmill—p. 12. Widow, Margaret Brodie. Children—

Aberdeen and Banff Wills.

1. Alexander ; 2. Hugh ; 3. James, appointed in will his executor ; 4. Mr. Thomas ; 5. Charles. 1. Elizabeth.

of Marjory, daughter of Andrew Moir of Overhill—
see p. 15.

1681. June 4. Robert Montgomerie in Pitgerso, a son bap.,
called Robert. Witnesses, Robert Montgomerie elder,
Robert Chein, and Robert Montgomery younger (Pitgerso or Pitgersie adjoins Greyshill).

1682. Janʸ 8. John Montgomery. Witness to the bap. of John,
son of George More, in the parish of Udny.

1683. June 21. Robert Montgomerie. Witness to the bap. of
Samuel, son of Andrew Moir—see p. 15.

1683. Decʳ 6. William Montgomery, at the Hill of Fiddes, has
Jean bap. Witnesses, William Crawford, William
Watson.

1684. John Montgomery, a child bap. in fornication, called
Gilbert. Witnesses, Gilbert Moir, Robert Montgomery,
younger.

1687. Novʳ 18. William Montgomery has Margaret bap. Witnesses, William Craighead and William Rainy.

Inferences.—As Robert Montgomery the elder was
a witness to the bap. of several of the children of Andrew
Moir and Agnes Montgomery, it is most probable he
was a near relation; probably Mrs. Moir's father or
brother.   *Ibid.*

1705. Janʸ 7. Alexander Black and Margaret Montgomery married. Marriages.
This had probably been a near relative of Alexander
Blake (so name is spelt in same register), who married,
27th July 1714, Agnes Steven (Stephen), and were
progenitors of the "Blacks of Wateredgemuir," in
Logie-Buchan. Thomas Black, who bought Wateredgemuir, married 10th July 1787 Mary Sangster (and was
succeeded by their eldest son, Thomas Black of Wateredgemuir, who married Margaret, daughter of Alexander
Innes of Clerkseat, Commissary of Aberdeen, father of
the late Alexander Black, of Hyde Park Terrace, London, who married Harriet, daughter of John S. Salt, J.P.
and D.L., of Weeping Cross, co. Stafford), and were the
grandparents of John Black, who married Elizabeth,
daughter of John Garden of Millfield, Aberdeenshire.
Their dau., Isobel Sarah Black, m. 1870 David Gill,
LL.D., of Blairythan—see p. 24.

G

SIMPSONS OF THORNTON, CONCRAIG, &c.

" Implebitur "—(It will increase).

The Simsons—Simpsons—Sympsons, &c., sons of Simon, are believed to have been originally Frasers of the Lovat family. Simon being the name of the first of them who settled in the Highlands, and a common name for their chiefs, they adopted the Gaelic designation of Mac-Shimei—that is, the sons of Simon—hence Simonson, Simson, or Simpson. A tradition which is preserved in an old branch of the Simpson family, long settled in the parish of Belhelvie, Aberdeenshire, from whom Simpson of Hazelhead, near Aberdeen, was descended, is to the effect that at a gathering in Inverness-shire, one Simon Fraser, hearing a piper play an obnoxious tune, slew him, and had to fly to the Lowlands, and was their ancestor.

The Simpsons of Idoch or Udoch, in the parish of Turriff, in Aberdeenshire, are stated to have owned that property from about the end of the 16th century. George Sympson of Udoch is Laird in 1649 (Acts of Parliament of Scotland, vol. vi., p. 192). Their arms in the Lyon Register are, argent, on a chief vert, three crescents of the first.[1] Crest, a Falcon. Motto—*Alis nutrior* (I am fed by birds). Robert Simpson of Thornton registers his arms, 1672-8, same as Idoch, but indents the chief as his difference; and for crest, a crescent or, and motto, *Implebitur*. Simpson of Hazelhead (descended of the Belhelvie family) bears as Idoch, within a bordure for difference; indeed all the Scotch families of the surname have their arms as "Idoch," with a difference. The late Sir James Young Simpson, Baronet, M.D., of Strathavon, Linlithgowshire, the most eminent person of the surname, bore, or, on a chief vert, a goshawk (the crest of Udoch) between two crescents argent.

I. Robert Simpson was Laird of Thorntoun, Lawellsyde, and Pittgavinie, in the parish of Bourtie, Aberdeenshire, prior to 6th Oct' 1669, in which year he is witness to a service—John Gordon of Bradlane (Broadland, near Huntly).—(Sheriff Court Records.) He registers arms as before stated, 1672-8, and is alive, resident,

Scottish Arms.

Poll-Book.

[1] Lindsay of the Mount, Lyon 1542, gives this coat for the surname of Symsoun, but a coat with the chief azure (*ibid.*) occurs 1508. The seal of George Symson, 1561, bears a fesse, instead of the chief, between three crescents. George Simpson of Udoch, 1672-8, was allowed the coat as in Workman, 1565-6. This Laird, with his wife, Jean Leslie, and family, appear as residing at Idoch, 1695-6.

and polled at Thornton, with his children, Robert, John, and Elizabeth, 1695-6—(Poll-book of Aberdeenshire, vol. i., p. 334), and was dead before 1729—(wife probably a Montgomerie, sister of Mrs. Moir, pp. 12 and 48). Issue—

1. Robert, his heir.
2. John, polled at Thornton 1695-6.
1. Elizabeth, born 1675, married 1699-1700, Andrew Moir, II. (of Cultercullen and Oldmill).—See that family, p. 17.

II. Robert Simpson, II. of Thornton, &c., succeeded before 1729; married   .   Issue (Bourtie Parish Register)—

1. Alexander, bap. 9th May 1713. Witnesses, Alexander Simpson of Concraig, in the parish of Skene (the child's uncle), and James Man, in the parish of Tarves.
2. Robert, bap. May 8, 1714. Witnesses, Alexander Gordon of Auchedie (Auchreddie), and John Symson, servitor to the Earl of Kintore (probably maternal and paternal uncles).
1. Mary, bap. Nov' 13, 1710. Witnesses, Alexander Simpson, in Mill of Kinguidy, and Robert Simpson, in Green of Udny.

III. Robert Simpson, III. of Thornton.

1. Helen, bap. 14th June 1744. Witnesses, John Leith of Blair and John Glenny.
2. Elizabeth, bap. 9th Feb' 1746. Witnesses, John Leith of Blair and John Glenny.

Probably this Laird married a Miss Leith of Blair, which is a property in the parish of Bourtie.

Alexander Simpson, in Mill of Kinguidy, Bourtie, a member of this family, had, according to the Bourtie Register, the following children baptized :—

1. James, 14th Jan' 1751.
2. Alexander, 20th Jan' 1753.
3. Peter, 28th Oct' 1761.
1. Janet, 11th Feb' 1750.
2. Jean, 3d Nov' 1755.
3. Elspet, 5th July 1759.

1716. Dec' 13. (Same Register.)—John Tower, in New Aberdeen, and Elizabeth Simpson, married.

SIMPSON OF CONCRAIG.

I. Alexander Simpson[1] (brother of Robert Simpson, I. of Thornton) was chamberlain to the Earl of Kintore, and in 1695-6 is polled as gentleman-tenant in Ardmurdo, parish of Kinkell, Aberdeenshire. He acquired, before 1713, the estate of Concraig, in the parish of Skene, in that county. Married Margaret Symsone.[2] Issue, at least one son and six daughters, viz. :—

 1. Patrick, designed younger of Concraig 1729, and Laird in 1741.
 1. Elizabeth.
 2. Helen ; married John Milne, in Brotherfield, in the parish of Peterculter, Aberdeenshire, and died 25th March 1752.[3]
 3. Anna.
 4. Margaret ; married the Hon. Major-General Mark Napier, fifth son of Francis, V. Lord Napier, and had issue.—(See Burke's *Peerage and Baronetage*, Art. Napier.)
 5. Katherine. (These five daughters, with their father and mother, are alive, and polled at Ardmurdo 1695-6.)

Poll-Book.

[1] Alexander Simpson, in Ardmurdo, had (Kinkell Register) the following children bap. :—

 1. Jean, 18th June 1706. Wit., Alex[r] Taylor, in Ardmurdo, and James Taylor, in Kinkell.
 2. Robert, 29th April 1708. Wit., Rob[t] Simpson of Thornton, and Mr. James Walker, in Peithill.
 3. Elspet, 20th Dec[r] 1718. Wit., Alexander Symson, in Belhelvie (this would almost point to a connection with the, at one time, numerous family of Simpson there, one of whom, Elspet Simpson, niece of Innes of Stow, m[d] Alexander Mitchell—(see p. 20), and Alexander Sangster, in Kinkell.
 Some of the other children had probably been born at Concraig.

[2] "1677. 8th June. Alex. Symsone, and Marg[t] Symsone, his spouse, resigned their rights in Lawelside, in Bourtie, to Rob[t] Sympsone of Thornton, for 3000 merks."—(Inverurie Court Books.) (See *Inverurie and the Earldom of the Garioch*, p. 329.)

[3] Mrs Helen Simpson or Milne, who d. 1752, has the following modest—ahem !—lines on her tombstone at Peterculter (Jervise's *Epitaphs*) :—

  "So, reader, underneath their lyes
  The virtuous, prudent, chaste, and wise,
  Of beauty great, and gentle blood,
  The darling of the neighbourhood.
  Think then of her bright, gentle soul,
  And first admire, and then condole."

6. Barbara; contracted 11th Jany 1730 to John Middleton, Register of St. Nicholas.
younger of Aberdeen, merchant, and had two daughters.
   1. Elizabeth Middleton; contracted 6th Augt 1759 to her
      relative, William Mitchell, Merchant Burgess of Aber-
      deen, whose first wife she was.—(See p. 20.)
   2. Janet Middleton; contracted 3d March 1766 to John *Ibid.*
      Ewen, of Aberdeen, Jeweller, author of the fine ballad,
      " Weel may the boatie row," whose only child
      1. Elizabeth Ewen, married 1787 a younger son of Grahame
         of Morphie, in Kincardineshire. Their son is Barron
         Graham of Morphie.

William Simpson, Baillie of Aberdeen (another brother of the *Ibid.*
first Lairds of Thornton and Concraig), married there, 11th Sept^r
1699 Mary, daughter of David Aedie of Newark and Easter-Echt,
Aberdeenshire (sister of Giles Aedie, wife of Alexander Skene,
XVIII. of that ilk), and had at least one daughter, Sarah Simpson,
II. wife of her cousin-german, George Skene, XIX. of that ilk.—
(See Douglas' *Baronage*, p. 36.)

Helen Simpson (a sister of the I. Thornton, &c.), married
James Coutts in Milnbrig. She is alive, and polled at Kirkstyle
of Cluny, with her daughter, Jean Couts, 1695-6 (Poll-Book of
Aberdeenshire, p. 225). Issue—1. James; 2. John, in Meikle
Finnersie of Echt (*Ibid.*, p. 210). 1. Jean.—(Sheriff Court Records
of Aberdeen, 13th July 1694.)

1658. June 18. Gilbert Coutts, in Finnersies, on the service of
              Patrick Dun, in the lands of Tartic, and heir of Dr.
              Robert Dun, deceased the night before, pp. 80-81.

1642. May 26. David Simpson, Burgess of Aberdeen, cautioner
              for Gilbert Coutts, in Finersie.

1608. Augt 23. David Symsone, Saddler in Aberdeen, cautioner
              for Robert Symsone, in Miltoune of Ashogle, parish of
              Turriff, which would almost point to a Turriff origin for
              the family.[1]

1729. .   .   The said day compeared judicially William Simp-
              son, late Baillie and Merchant in Aberdeen, Patrick

[1] *Inferences.*—That the Simpsons, so long connected with the Turriff
district, Lairds of Idoch there, &c., are the progenitors of the Thornton family,
as also of the large farming family of Simpson, long settled in the Belhelvie
district. George Simpson of Hazelhead, burgess cooper of Aberdeen, of the
last family, had several daughters; one of them married Turner of Menie;
another married one of the Bannermans of the Elsick family.

Simpson, younger of Concraig, Alexander Livingstone, Merchant in Aberdeen, curators elected, nominate, and chosen by Robert Simpson, now of Thornton, lawful son to the deceased Robert Simpson of Thornton.

The four above extracts are from the Sheriff Court Records of Aberdeen.

FORBES OF WATERTON, PARISH OF ELLON, ABERDEENSHIRE.[1]

" Virtute inimica quies "—(Inactivity is an enemy to virtue).

I. The first of this family was Thomas Forbes, who inherited Waterton from his father—(William Forbes of Tolquhon, in the parish of Tarves, Aberdeenshire, by his marriage in 1580 with J. Ogilvie of Banff. The Forbeses of Tolquhon, who were celebrated for their loyalty to the Stuarts, were one of the oldest and most influential branches of the noble family of Forbes) — married Jean, sister of Sir Gilbert Ramsay, Baronet, of Balmain, and was slain by the Kennedys of Kermuck 1652. Their son—

II. Sir John Forbes of Waterton, Knight, Hereditary Constable of Aberdeen (Patent Charles II.), mᵈ his cousin, 1663, Jean, sister of Sir George Gordon of Haddo, Baronet, afterwards Earl of Aberdeen; died 1675 (both children of Sir John Gordon, Bart., of Haddo), whose third son—

III. William Forbes, was in early life a medical practitioner in the town of Aberdeen (Poll-Book of Aberdeenshire, vol. ii., p. 632). Subsequent to 1695 Mr. William Forbes relinquished the medical for the clerical profession, and was for a long period, and up to the date of his death, Minister of Tarves, Aberdeenshire, a living to which he had been presented by his uncle on the mother's side, George, first Earl of Aberdeen. He mᵈ Janet, daughter of Professor James Gregory, inventor of the reflecting telescope.—(See family of Gregory, p. 63). Of this union fifteen children were born, who died either young or unmarried, except one son and four daughters, of whom the III., Jean Forbes, mᵈ 1737 the Rev. Andrew Moir (see p. 28). For the other three daughters of William Forbes and Janet Gregory see family of Gregory, p. 63. The son—

[1] For a more detailed account of this family *vide* Memorandum of the family of Forbes of Waterton, &c.

IV. James Forbes, M.D., of Aberdeen, married—first, Mrs. Helen Forbes, who died *s.p.* 1743; and secondly, Euphemia Rowe, whose son—

V. William Forbes of Echt and Springhill, Merchant in Aberdeen, had, by his marriage with Elizabeth, daughter of Dr. Thomas Arbuthnott of Montrose, younger brother of John, VI. Viscount Arbuthnott, with a son James Forbes, II. of Echt (of this family), and other issue, a daughter, Euphemia Forbes, married to her cousin, George Garden of Montreal, Merchant, p. 30.

Arms of Forbes of Waterton.—First and fourth, three boars' heads, couped, argent, muzzled, gules, for Forbes ; second and third, three unicorns' heads, erased, sable (for marrying Marjory, heiress of Sir Henry Preston of Formartine), by way of surtout, on an escutcheon argent, charged with a sword and key, saltier ways, gules, as Constable of Aberdeen.

ANDERSON OF FINSHAUGH.

" Stand sure."

(SKENE'S *History of the Highlands,* vol. ii., § 228.)

This surname, meaning literally the son of Andrew, denoting more probably a son of St. Andrew ; that is, a native Scotchman, as indicated by the cross of St. Andrew, the patron saint, in their shield. The Gaelic sept of Anderson are said to be an offshoot of the old potent stem of Clan Anrias, from which also sprang the Macandrews, MacGillanders, and the Gillanderes. One of the chief septs of this race were the Andersons of Candacraig, in Strathdon, Aberdeenshire, of which family there have been ten generations. The Andersons of Finshaugh derive from a very old burgess race of "Bon-Accord," and appear to be connected with the town of Aberdeen, holding important offices in it, so far back almost as any of the records of the town extend. [Jervise's "Epitaphs, &c."]

I. Gilbert Anderson, Burgess of Aberdeen, who died 2d Feb[y] 1598, m[d] at Aberdeen, 29th May 1576, Janet Moir, who d. 4th May 1601—(inscription on their tombstone given in Menteith's *Theatre of Mortality*)—and had at least three children, viz., [Reg. of St. Nicholas.]

David (of him again) and Christian[1] and Marjory Anderson—
(Marjory Anderson must have been a daughter by a former marriage, and thus only a half-sister of "Davie-do-a'-thing")—who
married Andrew Jameson, an architect of Aberdeen. Their son
was George Jameson, b. 1586, the celebrated painter, termed
"The Scottish Vandyke," who m[d], 12th March 1624, Isobel
Toasch, and had a large family, of which Mary Jameson married,
for her second husband, Prof. James Gregory.—See that family,
pp. 62-63.

DAVID ANDERSON, I. OF FINSHAUGH.

II. David Anderson (the son) was an eminent merchant of
Aberdeen, and acquired the estate of Finshaugh, or Finzeauch,
in the parishes of Keig and Tough, Aberdeenshire. His mathematical genius and taste for practical mechanics, and his ingenuity

Kennedy's
"Annals,"
&c.

in turning his skill to account on numberless occasions, won for
him the *sobriquet* of "Davie-do-a'-thing." His most notable
achievement seems to have been the removal, in 1610, of a large
rock known by the name of "Crag-Metellan," or Knock-Maitland,
which obstructed the entrance to the Aberdeen harbour. He
died 9th Oct[r] 1629. By his wife, Janet Guild, daughter of a
wealthy armourer of Aberdeen—probably of Matthew Gwill (or

St. Nicholas
Reg.

Guild), who was in 1596 "dekin of the Hammerman "—and
Mariane Ronaldsoun, m[d] at Aberdeen 6th Nov[r] 1570 (who died in
1667, having endowed a hospital at Aberdeen for the maintenance
and education of ten poor orphans), sister of the eminent Dr.
William Guild (sometime Principal and Lord Rector of King's
College, Aberdeen), he had, with other issue, a son David, who
succ[d] to Finshaugh, and died 19th Dec[r] 1643, whose representatives are the Bannermans, Baronets of Elsick, and a daughter,
Janet Anderson, m[d] the Rev. John Gregory of Drumoak ; and
from this lady the famous mathematical abilities shown by her
descendants are presumed to have come.

[1] 1613. 11th March.—David Anderson and Jean Guild had a daughter
Family Bible. Christian baptized.
1632. 24 Jan[r].—Christian Anderson, married George Wilson (eldest lawful
son of Duncan Wilson, merchant burgess of Aberdeen), who became "of
Finshaugh," and is represented by the Bannermans.—See *Burke's Peerage
and Baronetage*, &c.

The way in which this ingenious individual is said to have removed the rock Knock-Maitland, which in 1610 obstructed the entrance to the Aberdeen harbour, is as follows:—" He secured a number of empty casks to the block at low-water (presumably after it had been loosened), and when the flowing tide lifted the mass from its bed, he seated himself on one of the barrels, and, with colours flying, sailed up the harbour, amidst the acclamations of the delighted citizens." Anderson is believed to have put up the sun-dial now in the wall of the Town-House (or probably its predecessor) in 1597. Kennedy, in his *Annals of Aberdeen*, says, " He was also architect at constructing the steeple of St. Nicholas Church, and placed the weather-cock upon it with his own hands. —Council Reg., vol. xlviii., p. 469." *(margin: Dr. Joseph Robertson.)*

The picture of David Anderson (by his nephew Jameson) is now in the possession of his descendants the Bannermans, as is also an old chair, with his arms, &c. cut in high relief on it.

1536. 27th May. David Anderson, Burgess of Aberdeen, grants a perpetual annuity of £1 : 8s., arising from a tenement in the Upper Kirkgate, "moved by devotion, and for the good of his soul," to the Chantry and Altar of St. Salvator—Church of St. Nicholas. *(margin: Kennedy's "Annals," vol. ii., p. 22.)*

From Mortifications fixed up in Town-House, Aberdeen.

" 1640. Jean Guild, relict of David Anderson of Finach, Janet Anderson, spouse of Mr. John Gregory, minister at Drumeack, Wil. Thores, son to Mr. Tho. Thores, Minister at Udney, and Geo. Wilson, son to the deceased Geo. Wilson, Merchant Burges of Aberdeen, mortified the heritable and liferent right of the lands and tenements called the Black Friers Manse in Abd., with the barns yeards of the samen, with two tenements of land in the Castlegate of the said burgh, and 1700 merks Scots money, for maintaining ten orphans at schools or trades in the town of Aberdeen, whereof each orphan is appointed to have 50 merks Scots per annum."

" 1657. Alex' Anderson, elder, Burges of Aberdeen, mortified an hundred pounds Scotts to the said burgh, and an hundred pounds Scotts to the Gild Brethern Hospital, reserving the annual rent of both the said summs to himself during his life."—Arms, "Anderson of Finshaugh," see next page.

Alexander Anderson, D.D., Parson of Methlic and Vicar of Kinkell, Principal of the University 1550-8, and Mr. *(margin: Ibid., p. 269.)*

H

Andrew Anderson, Regent, in June 1569 deprived of their offices.

1537-40. Alexander Anderson, Sub-Principal of University.

Ibid.   Professors of Divinity. — 1704-10, George Anderson ; 1711-34, David Anderson.

Of the Finsaugh-Anderson family was—

Alexander Anderson—some say a brother, others say a cousin, of " Davie-do-a'-thing,"—born at Aberdeen near the close of the sixteenth century. He soon became known as an eminent mathematician, and was for some time a professor of mathematics at Paris. He published six thin quarto volumes, some of them exhibiting marked ability, and including the posthumous MSS. of Vieta, a celebrated geometrician, which he was chosen to edit.

David Anderson, who went from Aberdeen in the early half of the eighteenth century, and settled as a planter at Kingston, in the Island of Jamaica, was also of this family. He married, and had, with a son David and a daughter Mary, who both died unmarried, another daughter, Margaret Anderson, b. 1757, m^d 1782 Patrick Gill of Aberdeen ; their son was the late David Gill of Blairythan, &c.—See p. 24.

Arms—" ANDERSON OF FINSHAUGH."—Argent, a saltire sable, in chief a crescent gules, in sinister, dexter, and base a mullet gules (so depicted on roof of Town-Hall of Aberdeen).

" The saltire, or cross of St. Andrew's, evidently allusive to the name, is the principal change in 18 out of the 21 entries for the name in the Lyon Register."—*Scottish Arms*, p. 195.

THE GREGORIES OR MACGREGORS OF ABER-DEENSHIRE.

" Nec deficit alter ".—(Another succeeds).

The Gregories of Aberdeenshire, a family of which so many members were celebrated for their mathematical genius, settled in that county in or about 1624, and were originally Macgregors, and " counted kin" with the celebrated Rob Roy, to whom they were not very distantly related.

From the introduction to *Rob Roy*, first ed., pp. liv. to lix. :— " Rob Roy was sent by the Earl of Mar to Aberdeen to raise, it is believed, a part of the Clan Gregor, which is settled in that country. These men were of his own family (the race of the Ciar Mohr). They were the descendants of about three hundred Macgregors whom the Earl of Murray, about the year 1624, transported from his estates in Monteith to oppose against his enemies the Macintoshes—a race as hardy and restless as they were themselves. But while in the city of Aberdeen, Rob Roy met a relation of a very different class and character from those whom he was sent to summon to arms. This was Dr. James Gregory (by descent a Macgregor), the patriarch of a dynasty of Professors distinguished for literary and scientific talents, and the grandfather of the late eminent physician and accomplished scholar, Professor Gregory of Edinburgh. This gentleman was at the time Professor of Medicine in King's College, Aberdeen, and son of Dr. James Gregory, distinguished in science as the inventor of the reflecting telescope. With such a family it may seem our friend Rob could have had little communion ; but civil war is a species of misery which introduces men to strange bedfellows. Dr. Gregory thought it a point of prudence to claim kindred, at so critical a period, with a man so formidable and influential. He invited Rob Roy to his house, and treated him with so much kindness that he produced in his generous bosom a degree of gratitude which seemed likely to occasion very inconvenient effects. The Professor had a son about eight or nine years old—a lively stout boy of his age—with whose appearance our Highland Robin Hood was much taken.

" On the day before his departure from the house of his learned relative, Rob Roy, who had pondered deeply how he might requite his cousin's kindness, took Dr. Gregory aside, and addressed him to this purport :—' My dear kinsman, I have been thinking what I could do to show my sense of your hospitality. Now, here you have a fine spirited boy of a son, whom you are ruining by cramming him with your useless book learning, and I am determined, by way of manifesting my *great* goodwill to you and yours, to take him with me and make a man of him.' The learned Professor was utterly overwhelmed when his warlike kinsman announced his kind purpose, in language which implied no doubt of its being a proposal which would be, and ought to be, accepted with the utmost gratitude. The task of apology and explanation was of a most delicate description, and there might have been considerable danger in suffering Rob Roy to perceive that the promotion with which he threatened the son was, in the father's eyes, the ready road to the gallows. Indeed, every excuse which he could at first think of—such as regret for putting his friend to trouble with a youth who had been educated in the Lowlands, and so on—only strengthened the chieftain's inclination to patronise his young kinsman, as he supposed they arose entirely from the modesty of the father. He would for a long time take no apology, and even spoke of carrying off the youth by a certain degree of kindly violence, whether his father consented or not. At length the perplexed Professor pleaded that his son was very young, and in an infirm state of health, and not yet able to endure the hardships of a mountain life; but that in another year or two, he hoped his health would be firmly established, and he would be in a fitting condition to attend on his brave kinsman, and follow out the splendid destinies to which he opened the way. This agreement being made, the cousins parted, Rob Roy pledging his honour to carry his young relative to the hills with him on his next return to Aberdeenshire, and Dr. Gregory doubtless praying in his secret soul that he might never see Rob's Highland face again. James Gregory, who thus escaped being his kinsman's recruit, and in all probability his henchman, was afterwards Professor of Medicine in the College, and, like most of his family, distinguished by his scientific acquirements. He was rather of an irritable and pertinacious disposition ; and his friends were wont to remark, when he showed any symptoms of these foibles, 'Ah, this comes of not having been educated with Rob Roy.' "[1]

The connection between Rob Roy and his classical kinsman did not end with the period of Rob's transient power. At a period considerably subsequent to the year 1715, he was walking in the Castle Street of Aberdeen arm in arm with his host, Dr. James Gregory, when the drums in the barracks suddenly beat to arms,

[1] The first of these anecdotes, which brings the highest pitch of civilisation so closely in contact with the half-savage state of society, I have heard told by the late distinguished Dr. Gregory; and the members of his family have had the kindness to collate the story with their recollections and family documents, and furnish the authentic particulars. The second rests on the *recollections* of an old man who was present when Rob Roy took French leave of his literary cousin on hearing the drums beat, and communicated the circumstance to Mr. Alexander Forbes, a connection of Dr. Gregory's by marriage, who is still alive, 1829. The Gregories of Aberdeenshire descend from a common ancestor, with their famous kinsman, Rob Roy, viz., Dugald Ciar Mohr, or the great mouse-coloured man, a brother of Macgregor of that Ilk, or of Glenstræ, in Perthshire, chief of that ancient clan. *Temp.* James VI.

and soldiers were seen issuing from the barracks. "If these lads are turning out," said Rob Roy, taking leave of his cousin with great composure, "it is time for me to look after my safety." So saying, he dived down a close, and, as John Bunyan says, "went upon his way, and was seen no more."

GREGORIES OF KINNARDIE, &c., BANFFSHIRE, AND FRENDRAUGHT, &c., ABERDEENSHIRE.

"Altius"—(Higher).

Gregor Macgregor, fourth son of Gregor Macgregor, XII. of that ilk, who died about 1413, was ancestor of this family. Douglas' "Baronage," p. 496.

Their direct ancestor, who appears to have acquired considerable wealth, was—

I. James Gregory, Saddler, Burgess of Aberdeen, who was dead before 27th May 1623, when his son— Scott's "Fasti," part vi., p. 497.

II. The Rev⁴ John Gregory[1] was served his heir. In 162 Minister of Drumoak, in Aberdeenshire, "refusing to sign the Covenant, he fled to England, but, returning in June 1639, he was seized in bed on the night of the 2d June 1640 by a party of soldiers, carried before Gen. Monk, and fined. He was reponed, however, in 1641. He was again deposed in 1649, but the Synod *Ibid.* recommended that the sentence should be taken off. He did not long survive, and his son, Mr. Alexander, was served heir to his very considerable property 31st March 1651." His landed possessions were by no means small, viz., the lands and baronies of Kinnairdie, Conwath or Inverkeithnie, and also (I think) Netherdale, on Devronside, Banffshire, with the lands and barony of Frendraught, in the parish of Forgue, in Aberdeenshire. Mr. Gregory m⁴ Janet, dau. of David Anderson of Finshaugh (see p. 56), and by her had at least three sons and three daughters, viz. :—

1. Alexander, "Mr." of Netherdale, served heir at Banff to his father in the lands and barony of Conveth or Inverkeithnie, and the barony of Kinnardie, and fishings in the Deveron, &c.; also in the lands and barony of Frendraught. Index of Retours, 31st March 1651.

[1] Few men have produced so many talented and distinguished descendants, and I much regret having neither material nor space for a more full account of a family whose history is in every way so worthy of being recorded.

2. David "of Kinnairdie"[1]—best known by this designation—
succeeded to the large landed property of his elder
brother, b. 1627-8. Like so many of his family, he also
possessed a remarkable turn for mathematical and me-
chanical knowledge. This gentleman was twice married,
and had thirty-two children. He died about 1720.

Three of his sons were professors of mathematics at
the same time in three of the British universities, viz. :—

a. David (b. 1661, m[d] 1695 Elizabeth, dau. of Oliphant of
Langtown, M.A. of Baliol, 1692), at Oxford, and
Savilian Professor of Astronomy there; died 1710.

b. James, at Edinburgh.

c. Charles, at St. Andrews.

3. James (of him again).

1. Margaret, m[d] Baillie Mercer of Aberdeen, and had one son
and four daughters.

" Poll-Book,"
1695-6, vol.
i., p. 588,
and Burke's
" Landed
Gentry ;" art.
Irvine of
Drum.

2. Janet, m[d] Thomas Thomson of Faichfield, in Buchan, and
had three daughters — 1. Isobel (m[d] 1698 Alexander
Irvine of Crimond, afterwards of Drum, and had issue);
2. Janet; and 3. Margaret.

3. . . . (not known).

III. James Gregory, born Nov[r] 1638, F.R.S. 1668, &c., a
distinguished mathematician, and, excepting Newton, the greatest
philosopher of his age, was, about 1668, appointed Professor of
Mathematics at St. Andrews, and afterwards filled the same chair

Kennedy's
" Annals."

at Edinburgh. At the age of twenty-four he published *Optica*
Promota, a work of great merit, in which he announced the invention of the reflecting telescope. This being one of the most
valuable of modern discoveries, established his reputation in the
scientific world. After the publication of this work he visited
Italy, and resided for some years at Padua, where he published,
in 1667, *Vera Circuli et Hyperbolæ Quadratura*, which contained another discovery of his own, namely, the invention of an
infinitely conveying series for the areas of the circle of the hyperbole.[2] Prof. Gregory had not filled the Mathematical Chair at

---

[1] The Laird of Kinnairdie was also skilled in medicine and philosophy, and,
according to Hutton, was the first man in Scotland who kept a barometer,
a circumstance which nearly led to his being tried by the presbytery as a
wizard.

[2] For a particular list of his works and discoveries, see Hutton's *Philosophical*
and Mathematical Dictionary.

It is said that no less than sixteen members of this family have held British
Professorships.—(Chalmers' *Biographical Dictionary*, p. 289).

Edinburgh above a year, when, in Oct[r] 1675, being employed in showing some of his pupils the satellites of Jupiter through a telescope, he was suddenly struck with total blindness, and died a few days after, at the age of thirty-seven.[1] He married in 1669 his cousin Mary, dau. of George Jameson, termed by Walpole "the Scottish Vandyke," and widow of Burnett of Elrick (see p. 65), by whom he had a son and two daughters, viz. :—

1. James (of him again).
1. Helen, m[d] Alexander Thomson of Portlethen, and had issue.
2. Janet, m[d] the Rev[d] William Forbes, minister of Tarves, a younger son of Sir John Forbes of Waterton, on Ythanside (see that family, p. 54), and had, with others died young or unm.—
    1. James Forbes, Physician in Aberdeen, progenitor of the (last) "Forbes of Echt" family (see p. 55).
    1. Katherine Forbes, m[d] William Dyce, schoolmaster at Selkirk, and had issue.
    2. Nelly Forbes, m[d] the Rev[d] John M'Innes of Logie-Coldstone, and had issue.
    3. Jean Forbes, m[d] 1737 the Rev[d] Andrew Moir, and had issue (p. 28).
    4. Susan, b. 1716, m[d] 11th June 1751 the Rev[d] James Johnston (M.D. 1748) of Crimond. He died 1796, and she, who was the fifteenth and youngest child of her parents, 27th Dec[r] 1799.

IV. James Gregory, born 1674, Professor of Medicine in King's College, Old Aberdeen, where he founded the School of Medicine 1725-31. (His son John, M.D., filled the same chair from 1732-51, and again in 1755-66, along with Sir Alexander Gordon of Lesmoir.) He was twice married, and had several children, one of whom (the youngest of three children) was—

V. John Gregory,[2] M.D., an eminent medical and moral writer, and one of the most distinguished members of his illustrious family, b. at Aberdeen June 3, 1724, was some time first physician to His

[1] On account of his reputation and abilities an annuity of 800 merks per annum was settled at his death on his children, who were then very young, by Charles II., until the youngest should reach the age of sixteen.

[2] After filling in succession the Chairs of Philosophy and Medicine at Aberdeen, he was appointed in 1766 Professor of the Practice of Medicine in Edinburgh, and died in February 1773. His works were collected and published by Mr. Tytler (Lord Woodhouselee).

Majesty in Scotland, m⁴ 1752 the Hon. Elizabeth Forbes, dau. of the XIII. Lord Forbes. He was the intimate friend of the most eminent men of Edinburgh in its most brilliant period. Issue—

1. James (of him again).
2. William, Rector of St. Mary's, Bentham.
1. Dorothea, m⁴ 1782 the Rev. Archibald Alison[1] (of Balliol College, Oxford).
2. Margaret, m⁴ John Forbes of Blackford, Aberdeenshire, whose dau. m⁴ Wm. Moir of Park (p. 76).

VI. James Gregory, M.D. (of Edinburgh), an eminent physician and medical professor, b. at Aberdeen in 1753. He was twice married, and by his second wife—a dau. of Donald Macleod of Geanies—he had a large family.

Lyon Reg.

1766. John Gregory, M.D., F.R.S., &c., Professor of Medicine in the University of Edinburgh. Argent, a fir tree growing out of a mount in base, vert, surmounted, of a sword in bend, supporting an imperial crown in the dexter canton proper, and in chief and base a lion's head erased, azure, armed and langued, gules ; crest, a sphere ; motto, *Altius*.

GEORGE JAMESONE, Painter, b. 1587, ob. 1644.
"Sine metu"—(Without fear).

I. Andrew Jamesone, Burgess of Aberdeen, and an architect or builder in that town, m⁴ there in Aug⁴ 1585 Marjory Anderson, dau. of Gilbert Anderson, also a Burgess of Aberdeen—see p. 56.

Book of Bon-Accord, p. 134, &c.

1. Elizabeth, b. July 1586.
2. George, b. about 1587.

II. George Jamesone, portioner of Esslemont, born at Aberdeen about the end of the 16th century. "He was endowed by nature with an uncommon genius for portrait painting, which he discovered at an early period of life. After passing through the usual course of education at the schools and the college of the place, he went abroad and studied at Antwerp, being fellow student with Vandyke, under the celebrated Rubens. Returned to Aberdeen about 1620, where he prosecuted portrait painting. Married 12th March 1624 Isabel Toasch (who belonged to an old Burgess family of the town), by whom he had several sons and daughters. He was most celebrated as a portrait painter ; yet he not unfrequently applied his talent to minature, and also to

Kennedy's "Annals of Aberdeen."

[1] Prebendary of Sarum, and were the parents of Sir Archibald Alison, Baronet.

history and landscape painting. He painted many portraits of Charles I. and of James VI., as well as of the most of the eminent men who flourished in the beginning of the 17th century, and many of his works are to be found in the possession of the principal families in Scotland. The finest collection of his works is at Taymouth Castle, the seat of the Earl of Breadalbane, whose ancestor, Sir John Campbell of Glenorchy, had been the chief and earliest patron of Jamesone, who had accompanied him in his travels abroad." Jamesone is the first native Scotch painter on record, and is most justly termed "the Vandyke of Scotland." Jamesone died at Edinburgh in 1644, and was buried in Greyfriars' Churchyard there; but no memorial has been erected to his memory. All his sons died in early life, and he was survived by two daughters, viz. :—

1. Marjory Jamesone, m⁴ John Alexander, advocate in Aberdeen.
2. Mary Jamesone, m⁴—1st. . . . Burnett of Elrick; 2dly. Prof. James Gregory—see p. 63; and 3dly. George Ædie, Baillie of Aberdeen, the father of David Ædie of Newark, p. 53.[1]

"1653. 20th May. Who being solemnlie sworne upon their great oathes, affirmit that the deceast George Jamesone, painter, burgher of Aberdeen, and father to Marjorie Jamesone, spous to Mr. John Alex', Advocat, and to Marie Jamesone, bearers heirof, died last . . . vest and sast as of fee in all and haill the Mayns of Eslemont, with the manour-place, tour, fortalice, yardes, and pertinents of the same; in all the halfe toune and lands of Cowhills, with the pertinents, lyand within the barrony of Esslemonth and sheriffdome of Abd"; and that the said Marjorie and Marie Jamesones are the nearest and lawful heirs-portioners of their said deceast father in the lands and others foresaid." Sheriff Court Records of Aberdeen.

Mary Jameson (Mrs. Gregory) who appears to have inherited a portion of her father's genius, displayed her taste in needlework, and the fine tapestries which now decorate the east end of St. Nicholas Church, over the Magistrates' Gallery, were her work, viz., "Jephtha's Rash Vow," "Susannah and the Elders,' &c.

Arms.—Azure, a saltire or, cantoned with four ships under sail, argent.

[1] 1678. April 23. David Ædie, Baillie of Aberdeen, heir of George Ædie, his father in tenements in Aberdeen. Reg. of Sasines.

I

COPY of LETTER from MARY GRANT or LUMSDEN, Wife of the Revd JAMES LUMSDEN, Laird of Corrachree, in Logie-Coldstone, and Minister of Towie, both in Aberdeenshire—this Lady was a niece of the then "Grant of Ballindalloch"—to her Husband's Niece, addressed to Miss PEGGIE CATTANACH at Tillierey.

"TOWIE, *Monday, 5th Feb.* 1759.

" I got your letter, dear Peggie, on Saturday night last, and am very glade to fiend ye ar like to be seteled in a married state so much to the liking of your Good Lady and master. Provedence has always been very kinde to you in reasing up friends to you when ye was at a distance from your relations. I hope ye'll never forget to be thankfull to God for his Goodness to you and to your benefactors for theire kiendness. I'm willing to beleve that the yong man in your offer is as agreeable in behaveor as he is in circumstance, or Mr. and Mrs. Ligertwood wood give him no countenance. As ye have never been given to vainity, ye show'd at this time buy some Cloaths, useful and substansial, and continow to be a good manger, to make up for your want of money. I'll be glade to see you when its convenient. Mr. Lumsden and Nanie join me in compliments; and I am, D. P. (Dear Peggie), your affectionat friend and servent,"

(Sig^d)   " MARY LUMSDEN."

Margaret Cattanch, who m^d 1759 Andrew Mitchell, I. of Savock—see p. 22—was governess in the family and friend of James Ligertwood of Tillery, in the parish of Foveran—of the Cairnhill family, see p. 25—and his wife, Jean Robertson, sister of the I. Andrew Robertson of Foveran; their eldest dau., Margaret Ligertwood, m^d Sir William Seton, Bart., of Pitmedden.

————————

COPY LETTER, EARL MARISCHAL to Mr. MOIR, Minister at Peterhead—see p. 31—dated from Keithhall, 10th Octo' 1763.

" Sir—I have heard from all who know you so good a character of you, that I am glad the good Towne of Peterhead has you for minister, and I daresay you will be reciprocally pleased; be assured of the esteem with which, I am, Sir, your most humble servant,"

(Sig^d)   " MARISCHALL."

THE LATE PATRICK MOIR, Esq.

This highly respected gentleman, the eldest son of the Rev. Dr. Moir, of Peterhead, died at Calcutta more than two years ago. His friend and patron, Lord Minto, paid the last tribute to his worth in the following epitaph, in which his character and merits are most happily delineated [1] :—

Sacred

TO THE MEMORY

OF

PATRICK MOIR, Esq.,

Who died at Calcutta on the 5th of February
A.D. 1810,

IN THE 41ST YEAR OF HIS AGE.

In 1806 he filled the office of Secretary to Lord Minto, at that time President of the Board of Commissioners for the Affairs of India, whom he accompanied to Bengal in the year 1807, and was appointed Commissioner of the Court of Requests at Calcutta in the same year, a trust which he discharged with integrity, assiduity, and ability to the time of his decease.

His Virtues, Talents, and Accomplishments,
all of the highest order,
enhanced by a singular Simplicity
and Modesty of Character,
had attracted in an eminent degree
the Esteem and Regard
of the World.
His gentle but cheerful Manners,
his benevolent but warm Affections,
endeared him to numerous Friends,
Whose tender but sorrowful Recollections
will long survive him.
He lived respected and beloved,
and died deservedly and universally
deplored.

Soft on thy Tomb shall fond Remembrance shed
The warm but unavailing Tear ;
And purple Flowers, that grace the virtuous dead,
Shall strew the lov'd and honour'd Bier.

[1] *Aberdeen Journal.*

FAMILY OF WHITE.[1]

1. John White, born 12th June 1782, went from Bedfordshire and settled as a merchant at Quebec. He married Jane Macallum (born 26th July 1793, died 15th Feb[y] 1883), and died 26th Aug[t] 1827.

    1. Douglas - Leland, merchant, of Albany, married Sophia Horsley, and has issue.

    2. James, married, and is deceased, without issue.

    3. John, died young.

    4. Richard-Peniston, married (without issue).

    1. Maria, b. 15th Sept[r] 1815, married in 1838 Patrick Moir-Crane. See p. 39.

    2. Caroline, married John Gilmour, merchant, of Canada, and has issue.

    3. Henrietta-Helen, married Thomas Blatherwick, late Surgeon-Major in the Army, and has issue.

    4. Matilda, married first David Gilmour (brother of the above John Gilmour) of Quebec, merchant, and had issue; and secondly Farquharson Smith of Quebec, banker (without issue).

FAMILY OF BULTEEL.[2]

Three brothers of this surname came to England in 1600, after the "Revocation of the Edict of Nantes," and one of them settled in London, where he died unmarried; the other two in Devonshire, in which county they acquired the estate of Flete.

I. Edward Bulteel (a cousin of the late John Crocker Bulteel, M.P. of Flete, who married in 1826 Lady Elizabeth Grey, daughter of Charles Earl Grey) left England, and settled at Sligo in Ireland, at which place his Uncle Bulteel was Collector of the Customs. He married Eleanor Hume, of Scotch descent. Her mother, Susan Walker of Londonderry, was a descendant of General Walker, Governor of Derry. Issue—

    1. Edward-Josiah, D[r] 98th Reg[t], married Sarah Kelly of Dublin, and died without issue.

    2. Andrew-Hume; of him again.

    3. Samuel-William, of Manchester, Director of the Lancashire and Yorkshire Railway, died Nov. 1883, having married

[1] Arms of White of Holcott, Co. Bedford—Argent, a chevron between three wolves' heads erased, gules.

[2] Bulteel of Flete—Argent, a bend between fourteen billets, gules.

Elizabeth, dau. of Thomas Sharp of Manchester, engineer
(no issue).

1. Susan (died unm.)   2. Matilda, married (without issue).
3. Ellen.   4. Jane.
5. Margaret.   5. Anne.   6. Mary.

II. Andrew-Hume Bulteel was many years Collector of H.M.
Customs at Liverpool; married, 8th June 1841, Catherine, daughter
of Rev. Marcus Chartres, Prebendary of Clone and Rector of
Ferns, county Wexford, by his marriage in 1807 with Sophia
Irvin of Enniskillen, who was nearly related to the Humes and
Walkers before mentioned, and also to the Le Flemings of Rhydal,
in Cumberland.

Andrew-Hume Bulteel, of Liverpool, and Catherine Chartres.

1. Edward, b. Jany 1848,   } Tea Planters, India.
2. Andrew Mark, 29th Septr 1850, }
1. Sophia-Matilda, married, 11th Augt 1866, George Moir of
   Stoneywood, Manchester.—See p. 39.
2. Eleanor-Mary.   3. Emily-Catherine.

MOIR OF STONEYWOOD.[1]

The estate of Stoneywood, situated on the River Don, in Aber-
deenshire, four miles from the sea, consists of the properties of
Stoneywood, Waterton, Clinterty, and Greenburn, united in one
barony. It was originally the property of Fraser of Muckills, or
Muchalls, but was sold by Lady Fraser, in 1671, to John Moir of Tombstone
Kermuck, or Ellon (b. 1610, ob. 1671).   St. Nicholas,
                                                                Aberdeen.
The Moirs of Stoneywood seem, from the earliest record down
to their close, to have been devotedly attached to the House of
Stuart; and inherited, through Bishop Patrick Scougal, of Aber-
deen (the grandfather of Mary Scroggie, who married in 1683, as
first wife, James Moir, II. of Stoneywood), the Bible presented by
Charles I., when on the scaffold, to his faithful friend Bishop
Juxon. Bishop Juxon was, it is understood, a relative of the
Scougal family. The grandson of John Moir, I. of Stoneywood, was

James Moir, III. of Stoneywood, of whom, and his caird-
servant John Gunn, many amusing and interesting stories are told.

[1] For an interesting and beautiful account of this family, see "A Jacobite
Family" by John Brown, M.D. (the talented author of "Rab and his Friends"),
from which the particulars given are taken.

The best of these, perhaps, is the rescue of the Earl of Winton in 1715, then under sentence of death in the Tower for his concern in the Rebellion of that period. During his sojourn in the Tower, the authorities allowed his books and family papers to be carried to and from his cell in a hamper. Stoneywood, who happened to be in London with his servant, went to visit his captive friend. John Gunn, who was a man of immense size and strength, undertook, if the Earl put himself, instead of his charters, into the hamper, to convey him out of the Tower. This feat the stalwart Gunn performed with perfect success. Lord Winton retired to Rome, where he died in 1749. The son of this Laird,

James Moir, IV. of Stoneywood, born 1710, was one of the Stuarts' keenest supporters in the North, engaged ardently in the Royal cause, and raised the regiment known as "Stoneywood's," of which he was Lieutenant-Colonel. Defeated at Culloden, he, in common with his companions, was proscribed, and roamed for some time in the wilds of Aberdeenshire. An anecdote is told of his taking shelter with a cobbler named Clark, under the name of James Jamieson (a ready rendering of the son of James, his father), and acquitted himself so well in this new line of life as to win commendation from the old man, who said, "Jeemes, my man, what for did ye no tell me ye had been bred a sutor?" "And so I was freend," replied the Laird; "but to tell ye God's truth, I was an idle loon, gey weel-faured, and ower fond o' the lassies, so I joined the Prince's boys, and ye see what's come o't!" It is pleasant to add that Stoneywood, when brighter days came, never forgot the services of his old friends, and maintained the widow and five children of Bartlett (the cobbler in question) at Stoneywood, till the latter were able to support themselves.

After being assisted through many straits by his faithful wife, Margaret Mackenzie of Ardross, and his equally faithful servant, Gunn, who with his gipsy spouse, acted as messengers between husband and wife, Stoneywood followed his Prince's example, and escaped to Norway with some friends. He was protected by the King of Sweden, who conferred on him a patent of nobility; and, becoming a naturalised subject, his lady joined him within a year from his arrival at Gottenburg.

In Scotland, meanwhile, Moir was arraigned before the Edinburgh High Court of Justiciary; but even the testimony of adverse witnesses only went to prove the honour and humanity displayed throughout his soldier life, and he was allowed to return to Stoney-wood in 1762, where he died in 1782, leaving a widow and two daughters, his seven sons all having died before their father. Mrs. Moir survived till 1805, dying at the advanced age of ninety-six.

MOIR OF STONEYWOOD.

"Major opima ferat"—(Let the worthiest carry off the prize).

I. Johannes Moir, 1470-1516.   Reg. of the
    John Moore, Burgess of Aberdeen 24th July, 5 of James Great Seal,
    IV., whose son may have been.   2595, p. 551.

II. John Moir. He died before his son.

III. William Moir, Burgess of Aberdeen 1560, served heir to Skene's MS. John Moir, his grandfather. His son,

IV. Mr. William Moir, M.A., Burgess of Aberdeen, married Janet Rae, served heir to his father 1602, Treasurer of Aberdeen 1615.

    1. Henrie, bap. 28th May 1605.   Reg. of St.
    2. John, born 1610 (tombstone); of him again, as Stoneywood's Nicholas, Aberdeen.
        ancestor, next page.
    3. William, as Scotstoun's progenitor—see p. 75.
    4. Patrick, 13th July 1615, Baillie, and afterwards, 1648, Dean
        of Guild, and, 1672, Collector of Excise of Aberdeen,
        married 4th Jan^r 1637 Issobell Gray (twice in Register
        called Grahame). Issue—
        1. William, 7th June 1638.   2. Thomas, 20th May 1640.
        3. Patrick, 18th May 1641.   4. James, 22d July 1642.
        1. Issobell, 15th Dec. 1646.   2. Jean, 25th June 1648.
        3. Elspeth, 10th June 1652.   Sir Robt Farquhar, John Leslie,
          y^r, &c., Godfathers.
        4. Rachel, 25th March 1655.   5. Margaret, 10th March 1659.
    5. George.

V. John Moir, I. of Stoneywood (eldest son of Mr. William Tombstone Moir, Burgess of Aberdeen, and Janet Rae), born 1610, is said, St. Nicholas Churchyard, according to Skene's MS., to have been first designed of Ferryhill, Aberdeen.

afterwards of Kermuck or Ellon, and in 1671, as before stated, of Stoneywood.

"1657. The two Kennedys, flying the country, make over their estates to John Moir, and his wife, J. Sandilands, and the longest liver of them, p. 6. He has a charter of Cairnmucks in 1665."

Memoranda of the Family of Forbes of Waterton, 1857.

"1668. John Moir and his wife make over to Sir John Forbes of Waterton all the lands of Ardgrain, Cairnmucks, Broomfield, Kirkhill, and other property they had bought from the Kennedies for £42,500 Scots, p. 8." By which it would appear the estate of Ellon had only been held by John Moir for eleven years. He married Jean Sandilands (b. 1636, died 5th Augᵗ 1687), eldest dau. of James Sandilands, I. of Colton, by Marjory Burnett of Countesswells—see that family in sequel. (Jean Sandilands married, secondly, on Stoneywood's death, William Cumine of Auchry, and had issue),

1. James, 1659.
2. John, according to Skene's MS., Civilist of King's Coll., and an Advocate in and Town-Clerk of Aberdeen, 1689, died young.
3. William, 15th Janʳ 1669. Dr. Wm. Moir, Dr. Wm. Johnston, Dr. Wm. Fraser, and William Gellie, godfathers—first of the Moirs of Invernettie, p. 77.
4. Patrick, bap. Decᵗ 12, 1671.
1. Issobell, 31st Augᵗ 1660.
2. Mariorie, 5th Jany. 1665.
3. Jean, 21st Octʳ 1673.

According to the genealogy of the family of Sandilands of Craibstone and Cotton, Alexander Moir (fourth son of the above John Moir and Jean Sandilands) was Professor of Greek in the Marischal College of Aberdeen.

Forster's Members of Parliament, p. 253.

VI. James Moir, II. of Stoneywood, bap. at Aberdeen 1st Septʳ 1659, Joⁿ Jaffray, Provost, James Moir, Mr. Jaˢ Sandilands, &c. godfathers, who sat in Parliament for fifteen years as Member for Aberdeenshire, 1689-1702, 1702-1707; was also one of the Commissioners appointed for settling the Union of the Kingdoms; died 22d Novʳ 1739.

And Tomb-Stone St Nicholas.

James Moir, married first, 10th July 1683, Mary, eldest dau. of the Rᵗ Revᵈ William Scroggie, Bishop of Argyll (elected 1666, died 1675), by his wife, a dau. of Patrick Scougal, Bishop of Aberdeen, who was a son of Sir John Scougal of that Ilk, in East Lothian.

1. James, his heir.
2. Rhoderick, bap. at Aberdeen 25th Augt 1689, whose portrait,
     clad in armour, is amongst the Stoneywood pictures;
     drowned at sea along with his cousin James Sandilands,
     1713-14.
3. William, an Advocate (?), and probably the inheritor of the
     estate of Whitehill, in Midlothian, a property which had
     devolved by inheritance from the Scougal family to that of
     Stoneywood.
4. Alexander, Principal of St. Andrews Coll. at the abolition of
     Episcopacy, whose descendants are stated to have inherited
     the estate of Invernettie, in Buchan—see Moir of Inver-
     nettie, p. 77.
   1. Jean, married John Abernethy, II. of Mayen—see p. 83.
   2. Katherine.
   3. Marjory.

VI. James Moir, II. of Stoneywood, married, secondly, Jean,
dau. of Alexander Abernethy, I. of Mayen, and relict of William
Moir of Scotstown—see p. 75.

   1. William, of Lonmay—see that family, pp. 77-8.
   2. John, b. 1697, died 19th April 1720.
   3. Patrick, 26th Feb. 1707. Alex^r Moir, Regent, a witness.
   1. Janet, married 14th June 1733 Patrick Byres, I. of Tonley—
       see that family.
   2. Isabella, died unmarried.

VII. James Moir, III. of Stoneywood (eldest son of James
Moir, by his first wife, Mary Scroggie), one of the keenest of the
Stuarts' supporters in the North; engaged ardently in the royal
cause; raised, and was the Colonel of "Stoneywood's" Regiment;
and, as before stated, married Jean, daughter of William Erskine
of Pittodrie, by his wife, Mary Grant of Ballindalloch; and died
1782. Issue, five sons and two daughters.

   1. James, his heir, b. 1710.
   2. Thomas, who having had a quarrel with his brother James
       when they were both young men, took it so much to heart
       that he left his father's home clandestinely, and went to
       sea, having engaged himself as a sailor. He afterwards
       settled as a merchant in Falmouth. Issue—1. Capt
       Thomas; 2. James, a Barrister; 3. A dau., m^d Dr Vivian
       of Falmouth.

K

Skene's MS. James Moir, IV. of Stoneywood, having lost his own seven sons, "was very anxious to form a nearer connection by the marriage of his daughter Maria to her cousin James Moir (the Barrister). He intended to have paid a portion to his elder daughter Mrs. Skene, and to settle the estate of Stoneywood on James Moir and his daughter Maria, which upon the eve of accomplishment was defeated by the underhand machinations of Mr. Durno—see sequel—the as yet unrevealed enemy of the family, who feared that the marriage might become the means of bringing his base practices to light. Accordingly he found means to persuade Mr. James Moir that his uncle was deceiving him, and had given a false statement of his affairs, as the estate was drowned in debt, and he only wanted by the marriage to involve Mr. James Moir in his toils, so as to get him to relieve the burdens on the property. Upon obtaining this information the young gentleman thought it prudent to leave Aberdeen, and when he reached England wrote to his uncle stating the cause of his desertion. Miss Moir felt it very severely for a long time, and the disappointment occasioned her withdrawing herself much from society; while her father was so offended as to revive again the disunion which had so long separated the two families."

3. Alexander; 4. William,—both d. abroad unm.; 5. Charles engaged in the Rebellion of 1745. 1. Mary; 2. Clementina, named after Queen Clementina Sobiesky, mother of Prince Charles Edward.

"1745. In the beginning of November Lord Lewis Gordon, Kennedy's "Annals of Aberdeen," vol. i., p. 229. who had been appointed by the Prince Lord Lieutenant of the counties of Aberdeen and Banff, made his appearance in the town, accompanied by William Moir of Lonmay, and James Moir of Stoneywood, and assumed the direction of public affairs."

IV. James Moir, IV. of Stoneywood, b. 1710, married at Ardross, in Ross-shire, in Sept' 1740, his cousin Margaret, daughter of   Mackenzie of Ardross; and had fifteen children, who mostly died children, excepting Charles (the eighth son), b. 1752, entered the British Army, and was killed in America.[1]

1. Jane married George Skene of Rubislaw, whose descendants now represent this family.
2. Maria married Major Ramsay of the Scotch Brigade, a son of Ramsay of Kinaldie, in Forfarshire (without issue).

This Laird was, like his progenitors, a warm supporter of the Stuarts.

[1] Arms—see p. 46.

MOIR OF SCOTSTOWN.

" Non sibi sedi cunctis "—(Not for self, but for all).

V. William Moir (whom I make third son of Mr. William Moir,
Burgess of Aberdeen, and Janet Rae—see p. 71), I. of Scotstown,[1] Professor in Marischal College, Aberdeen. Married Jean,
dau. of Gilbert Gordon of Gordonsmill, and had a son.   Skene's MS.

VI. Dr. William Moir, II. of Scotstown, married at Dyce 5th
June 1656 Margaret,[2] dau. of Gilbert Skene of Dyce; and died
1670. Issue—

    1. William, his heir, bap. 9th Sept' 1658. Ro. Forbes, Bailie,
        Gilbert Skene of Dyce, Mr. Wm. Moir Principal, Pat' Moir,
        late Bailie, Alex' Skene of Dyce, yo', Mr. John Campbell,
        &c., godfathers.

    2. Gilbert, 15th Feb' 1663, went to Poland 1667.

    3. Patrick, 10th Aug' 1666.

    4. Alexander, 8th May 1668.

    1. Jean, 11th June 1657. Patrick Moir, Bailie, and Gilbert
        Skene of Dyce, godfathers.

    2. Margaret, 15th Dec' 1659.

    3. Marjorie, 22d May 1661.

    4. Jean, 25th April 1670.

    5. Issobell, 24th Dec' 1671.

    6. Marie, 8th Oct' 1676.

    7. Elizabeth, 11th April 1680. Ja' Moir and Mr. Rob' Patrie,
        of Portlathan, godfathers.

VII. Dr. William Moir, III. of Scotstown, b. 1658, married
Jean, dau. of Alexander Abernethy, I. of Mayen—see p. 82; she
remarried, as his second wife, James Moir, II. of Stoneywood—see
p. 73. His son—

VIII. Alexander Moir, IV. of Scotstown, was served heir to his
father 26th Jan' 1695; married Mary Chalmers.   Retours and
                                                   Reg. of St.
1721. Aug' 19. "Alex' Moir of Scotstoune, and Mary Chalmers, Nicholas.
    his sp., a da., Janet, bap'. James Moir of Stoneywood,
    and Dr. Patrick Chalmers, physician, witnesses."

---

  [1] The estate of Spittal seems also to have gone along with that of Scotstown in the Moir family.

  [2] She is alive 1695-6, and polled with her daughters Jean and Elizabeth.   Poll-Book, vol.
                                                                                ii., p. 607.

1723. March 4. Jean, bap^d. Wm. Moir of Innernethy, and James
    Moir, merch^t, witnesses.
1724. May 16. William, bap^d. Wm. Moir, son to James Moir of
    Stoneywood, a witness. Their son—

IX. George Moir, V. of Scotstown, married twice. By his first
wife he had—

    1. Alexander, his heir.
    George Moir married, secondly, Margaret, dau. of George
        Cumine of Pittulie, by his wife and cousin, Christian
        Guthrie, of King-Edward. Issue—

Tombstones
in vault
St. Peter's
Churchyard,
Aberdeen, &c.

    2. George Charles, b. 10th Octr 1771, sometime merchant in
        Bahia, afterwards of Denmore, near Aberdeen; died
        1851, having married Mary Agnew, only dau. of the late
        Sir William Bruce, IX. Bart. of Stenhouse. Issue, two
        daughters—

        1. Mary Anne Moir, married the late Lieut.-Col. Knight
            Erskine of Pittodrie. Issue, the present Laird,
            and a daughter, Mrs. Flower.
        2. Margaret Isabella Moir, married Joseph Dundas of
            Carron Hall and Fingask, Stirlingshire, and has
            issue.

    3. William, b. 1789, of Park, on Deeside, married Mary Eliza-
        beth (who d. 1868), dau. of John Forbes of Blackford, by
        Margaret Gregory—see p. 64; and died 1843, leaving
        five sons and five daughters, of whom—

        1. George, as VIII. of Scotstown.
        1. Mary Christina, married, 1795, Alexander Fraser,
            IV. of Fraserfield or Balgownie, of the noble
            family of Saltoun, and had issue.
        2. Isabella, married John Urquhart of Craigston, and
            had issue.

X. Alexander Moir, VI. of Scotstown, b. 1764, for many years
Sheriff-Substitute of Aberdeen; d. 21st June 1824, having married
Margaret, dau. of James Gordon of Leicheston, in Morayshire,
and had by her an only daughter.

XI. Isabella Moir, VII. of Scotstown, b. 14th May 1799,
married 10th June 1822 Sir Michael Bruce, VIII. Bart. of Stenhouse; and died 19th Novr 1867 (without issue).

XII. George Moir, C.B., Col. Bengal Horse Artillery, b. March 1820, VIII. of Scotstown (eldest son of William Moir of Park, and Mary Elizabeth Forbes), succeeded to that property under the will of his cousin the above Lady Bruce ; married Miss Bean, dau. of Col. Bean, and died in India 5th Feby 1870, whose son,

XIII. William Moir, IX., and now of Scotstown, is a Lieut. in the 18th Hussars.

Arms, p. 46.

MOIR OF INVERNETTIE.

"Deus dedit"—(God gave).

This family was a cadet of Moir of Stoneywood, and the estate, which is near Peterhead, reverted back to that family on the extinction of the Invernettie line.

James Moir of Invernettie matriculates arms in 1792—see p. 46. His wife probably was Catherine Arbuthnot, as a James Moir of Invernettie marries a sister of John, VI. Viscount Arbuthnot.

William Moir (fourth son of John Moir of Stoneywood, and Jean Sandilands), a merchant in Aberdeen, bought the estate of Invernettie. There is a charter to William Moir, dated 1708, merchant in Aberdeen, of the lands of Invernettie. Mr. Moir was succeeded in this estate by his nephew. *Sandilands' "Genealogy," and Skene's MS.*

1720. 21st Dec^r. "William Moir of Innernethie, a wit. to the bapt. of William, son of Dr. Mathew M'Kaill, physician, and Marg^t Black, his spouse." *Reg. of St. Nicholas.*

MOIR OF LONMAY, AFTERWARDS OF NEW GRANGE.

I. William Moir,[1] first of the Moirs of Lonmay, in Buchan (was eldest son of James Moir, II. of Stoneywood, by his second wife,

---

[1] "The estate of Whitehill, Midlothian, had come into the Stoneywood family through inheritance from the Scougals. The Laird seems to have given it to his son William, who, in 1727, has a charter of it, and is styled William Moir of Whitehill, and by a second charter, dated 1732, this William seems to have disposed of Whitehill and purchased Lonmay."

Jean Abernethy—see p. 73). He married a sister of General Fullerton of Dudwick.

1. William, his heir.

1. Isabella.   2. Catherine.

3. Jean, married William Cumine of Pittulie, in Buchan, and by her had Captain Adam Cumine, first of the Cumines of Rattray, near Peterhead.

Douglas's "Baronage.' Skene MS. Most of particulars about this family taken from it.
II. William Moir, II. of Lonmay, sold that property and bought New Grange, in Forfarshire. He married Wortley, eldest dau. of James Stuart of Blairhall, of the noble family of Bute. Issue—

1. William.

2. James.

1. Mary.   2. Margaret.

3. Anne.

III. William Moir of New Grange married. Issue—

1. William.

2. George.   3. Alexander.

And five daughters, one of whom, Wortley Cornelia Anne Moir, was second wife of Sir James Gardiner - Baird, V. Baronet.

"Captain Moir, lately (1837) tried and executed in London for having shot a person who was trespassing in his grounds, near London, was the representative of this family."

MOIR OF HILTON.

"Virtute non aliter"—(By virtue, not otherwise).

Reg. of St. Nicholas, Aberdeen.
I. William Moir, Advocate in Edinburgh, married 21st May 1666 Isobel, dau. of John Alexander, burgess of Aberdeen, and was admitted in Sept' 1670, *jure paternitatis*, burgess of Aberdeen. In 1666 he bought the lands of Knaperna, in Udny parish; 1668 those of Fisherie in King-Edward, probably from the Guthries of King-Edward; and in 1674, from the Donaldsons of Hilton, those of Hilton in Ellon parish, all in Aberdeenshire. Between 1672-3 Lyon Reg. he matriculates arms, and is designed "of Hilton"—see p. 46. About 1682 he sold Hilton to the Roses of Insch, who gave it the name of Rosehill. This family again sold it, about 1693, to the Turners—a family whose progenitors were farmers in the parish of Birse, Aberdeenshire, who gave it its present name of Turnerhall. William Moir, who was one of the Principal Clerks of Session, was M.P. for Kintore 1667; Convention 1669-74.

1672. 5th July. "He was, by order of the Parliament, sent to prison in the Tolbooth of Edinburgh," during the Lord Commissioner's pleasure, "for some words uttered by him tending to the subversion of the constitution of Parliament. He was released on the 10th, having craved pardon of the Commissioner and the Parliament on his knees." Issue— Forster's Members of Parliament, p. 253.

Skene's MS.

1. William, b. 1667.
2. James, b. 1670; godfather, James Moir of Ferriehill.
3. William, b. 1671; godfathers, Dʳ Wm. Moir of Scotstoun and Wm. Moir, his son.
4. George, b. 1688.
1. Jeane, 20th June 1673; John Moir of Barnes, a godfather. Reg. of St. Nicholas.
2. Anna, 4th July 1683, after Anna, Countess of Aberdeen, and Lady Anna Gordon, dau. of Sir George, Earle of Aberdeen, and Lord High Chancellor of Scotland. Mr. Wm. Moir, Dʳ of Medicine, John Moir, Apothecarie, Sir Geo. Skene of Fintray, godfathers.

MOIR OF BARNES.

"1678. 2d April. Walter Reid comperit for John Moir of Barnes, and produced ane charter grantit be ye Earl of Mar in favour of Alexander Erskine of Barnes, predecessor of the said John Moir, dated 22d July 1636." Sheriff Court Records of Aberdeen.

I. John Moir of Barnes, in the parish of Premnay, Burgess of Aberdeen, married 13th Febʸ 1655, at Aberdeen, Marie, or Mary, Cochran. She had doubtless been a Cochran of Dumbreck.[1] Registers of St. Nicholas.

1. Johne, 18th Septʳ 1660. 2. Walter, 14th Novʳ 1661.
3. Johne, 21st April 1663. 4. William, 2d March 1666.
1. Janet, 22d Novʳ 1665; Wm. Moir and Dr. Wm. Moir godfathers.

[1] The Cochrans of Dumbreck were long connected with the town of Aberdeen. Walter Cochran of Dumbreck, see p. 21, was its Provost 1691-93; and his son, Walter Cochran, was Town-Clerk-Depute in 1728. They intermarried with the old Gordons of Newton, Cruickshanks of Banchory, Udneys, &c. Kennedy's "Annals of Aberdeen."

Arms.—Ermine, on a chief, gules, a stag's head erased or, between two mullets argent. Lyon Register.

2. Marjorie, 12th March 1657, became second wife of George
   Gordon, II. of Sheelagreen.
3. Marie, 20th Jany 1659; Mr. John Campbell, &c., godfathers.
4. Isobel, 7th June 1664.
5. Agnes, 20th April 1667.
6. Jean, 9th July 1668.
7. Margaret, 11th Novr 1669.
8. Christian, 4th July 1671.
9. Mary, 26th April 1673.

Index of Retoura.

"1674. April 11. Janet, Marjory, Isobel, Agnes, Jean, Margaret,[1]
   Christian, and Marie Moires are served heirs-portioners
   of John Moir of Barnes, Merchant Burgess of Aberdeen,
   their father."

Poll-Book, vol. ii., p. 623.

"Mary Cochran, relect of the deceast umquhill John Moir,
sometyme of Barnes," is alive 1695-6."

MOIR OF FERRYHILL.

I. James Moire, who has in 1667 a lease of Ferryhill (but is
sometimes described of Ferryhill), married, first, I think, Jeane
Moire.

Reg. of St. Nicholas.

1. William, 8th Feby 1666; Dr. Wm Moire, Mr. Wm. Moire,
   Advocat, and Robt Burnet, godfathers.

Retours.

2. James, 19th Jany 1667, Professor of Philosophy in Marischal
   Coll. "1696, April 2d, served heir of John Moir, in
   Ferrihill, his father.
3. John, 19th Decr 1668.
1. Marjorie, 24th Decr 1669.

Memoir of Sir P. Dun.

James Moir married, secondly, Rachell, dau. of Charles Dun,
Litster, of Aberdeen, sister of Sir Patrick Dun, Court Physician,
at Dublin, and niece of Dr. Patrick Dun, Principal of Marischal
College, the munificent founder of the Grammar School of Aber-

[1] Margaret Moir seems to have married Captain James Gordon, designed
"of Barnes," p. 96.

deen. The Dunns of Tarty, in the parish of Logie-Buchan, were near relatives of this family (p. 53). James Moir and Rachel Dune had

1. Janet, 21st Jan^r 1673; Robt Forbes, Provost, Thos Mitchell, late Bailie, &c., godfathers.
2. Margaret, 28th Jan^r 1674; John Moir of Stonniewood, Pat^k Gellie, &c., godfathers.
3. Catherine, 5th Octr 1676. 4. Isobel, 1684. Ja^s Moir of Stoneywood, Mr. Ja^s Sandilands of Craibstone, Mr. Walter Grahame, Robt Burnet of Elrick, godfathers.

Rachell Dune or Moire, with her two daughters, Catherine and Janet, are polled 1695-6. Poll-Book, vol. ii., p. 625.

MOIR OF OTTERBURN.

"Mediocriter"—(With moderation).

I. Mr. Thomas Moir, minister of Morebattle 1610-33, second son of Moir of Abergeldie, co. Aberdeen, married Isabel Ker.

II. Mr. William Moir of Otterburn, in the parish of Morebattle, was served heir of his father 29th October 1639. He acquired Corbethouse; it came into the possession of his widow, Dorothy Ker, 18th September 1673, who married, 6th October 1672, Mr. William Galbraith, minister of Morebattle, and afterwards of Jedburgh, and he disponed Corbethouse to her son 9th April 1687.

III. Thomas Moir of Otterburn and Corbethouse registered arms about 1676, and three sons—Thomas, Andrew, Henry.

IV. Thomas Moir of Otterburn died in May 1756, was succeeded by his son.

V. Andrew Moir of Otterburn, who married Elizabeth Elliott, and had a son.

L

VI. Thomas Moir of Otterburn, whose estates were sold by judicial sale 4th December 1765, Otterburn to Gilbert Elliot in Jedburgh, Corbethouse to William Ker of Gateshaw, and Rannieston to Adam Keir, baker in Edinburgh; he was dead *s p.* before 23d July 1783, when his sisters Sarah, Jean, Barbara, Charlotte, Christina, and Elizabeth were his coheirs of provision general.

Arms, p. 47.

ABERNETHY OF MAYEN.[1]

"Salus per Christum"—(Safety through Christ).

I. Alexander Abernethy (a cadet of the Abernethies, Lords Saltoun) of Auchencloich, in the parish of Rothiemay, Banffshire, m[d] Isobel, contract dated 30th Nov[r] 1658, dau. (and co-heir with her sisters Christian Hacket, wife of Robert Gordon of Chapeltoune, and Elizabeth Hacket, of Archibald Dunbar of Newton), of Walter Hacket and his wife Jannet Leslye, who had a charter of the lands of Mayen in 1649. Mr. Abernethie bought up the interests of his sisters-in-law in Mayen, and became sole proprietor. Issue—

1. John, his heir.

2. William.   3. "Master" George.

1. Jean or Joan, m[d], first, William Moir of Scotstoun, see p. 75; and secondly, James Moir of Stoneywood, see p. 73.

2. Christian, m[d] Alexander Hay of Arnbath, who also owned the estate of Tonley; from him it was bought by the ancestors of the Byres family, 8th April 1720. Mr. Hay engaged in the Rebellion of 1715, and was forfeited, although he had a family of eight children; his descendants are now extinct.

[1] Most of the facts about the Abernethys of Mayen were sent me by Captain Dunbar Dunbar of Sea Park, and were taken by him from original documents in the Mayen charter-chest.

In two documents therein is mentioned—"1643, 4th July. Captain Thomas Moore, son of the deceased Thomas Moore in Peterhead, when James Abernethie, servitor to Mr Robert Bruce. Advocate, is appointed actor, factor, and commissioner for him."

1644, 20th July.—Thomas Moore is designed "Generall-Adjutant of ye Scots Cavilrie" in England, when he gives full power to James Abernethie, Writer and Advocat, to arrest James Ore (Orr) in the Canongate.

3. Janet.   4. Elizabeth.

5. Isobel, m^d the Revd Alexander Shand of Insch.

Alexander Abernethie died 1683, and his widow, Isobel Hacket, thereafter married Alexander Forbes of Blacktoune.

II. John Abernethy, II. of Mayen, m^d Jean, dau. of James Moir, II. of Stoneywood, by his first wife, Mary Scroggie, see p. 73, while his sister, Jean Abernethie, is the second wife of his father-in-law.

1. James, his heir.

1. Jean or Joan, m^d Dr. William Moir of Spittel, see p. 75.

2. Elizabeth, m^d the Revd Hugh Innes of Mortlach.

III. James Abernethy, III. of Mayen, married Jane, daughter of Alexander Duff, I. of Hatton. Having unfortunately shot John Leith of Leith Hall in a duel fought in the streets of Aberdeen in Decr 1763, he fled to the Continent, and was outlawed. For an account of this duel, see sequel. Issue—

1. James, his heir, IV. of Mayen, died unm. and intestate 1785, and four daughters, viz. :—

1. Jane (b. 1751, d. 1805), m^d Major, afterwards Colonel Alexander Duff, 58th Regiment, generally known as "Tiger Duff," so called from a deep seam in his face, inflicted in an encounter in India with a tiger. Their son, Captain William Duff of Mayen, sold that property ; d. 1857.

2. Isobel, m^d Captain William Graham, 42d Reg^t, sometime "Master of Ceremonies at Edinburgh" (Skene MS.)— and had issue.

3. Helen.   4. Anne.

Arms.—Or, a lion rampant, gules, surmounted of a ribbon, sable.
Crest.—A parrot feeding on a bunch of cherries, proper.

MOIRS.[1]

From Registers of St. Nicholas, Aberdeen, 1570-1700.

1570. Feby 4. James Kay and Margaret Moir married.

1571. Feby 17. Eyngane Alexander and Janett Moir married.

1575. Augt 14. Robert Boyd and Janett Moir married.
    1. Archibald, 14th Augt 1575.

1574. June 20. Walter Moir and Crichton Paterson married.

1574. Augt 24. John Fiddes and Marione Moir married.

1575. Decr 4. Richard Moir and Nans Fresar have a dau. Nans baptized.

1578. March 3. John Groitt and Margaret Moir married.

1587. July 25. John Moir and Margaret Paip married.

1579. Novr 8. Wm. Carmyshell and Marg^t Moir have Alexander baptized.

1581. Jany 11. Thos. Cowper and Kathrin Moir have a dau. baptized.

1583. Septr 15. Wm. Moir and Cristian Moreson have Alexander baptized.

1607. Decr 27. Patrick Ferguson and Katherine Moir married.

1588. May 17. Alexander Moir and Elspet Chein have Patrick baptized.

    Patrick or Peter Moir and Elspet Annand have—
        1. Margaret, 24th Novr 1632; 2. Alexander, 8th Jany 1635; 3. John, 7th April 1637; 4. William, 18th July 1641—Thos. Boyes, &c.; 5. A son (blank), 17th July 1644.

1604. Feby 21. Walter Moir, a dau. baptized, name blank.

1609. Feby 7. Alexander Moir and Agnes Wilson married.

---

[1] The author hopes this register will be of use in assisting families descended from the Aberdeen Moirs in tracing their pedigree.

  I would much have liked to have followed out, as far as possible, a detailed history of the families mentioned in St. Nicholas Register, but have neither space nor material to do so.—A. J. M. G.

1612. April 21. John Moir and Margaret Anderson married.

Arthor Moir and Cristian Wricht.
    1. Elspet, 18th Sept' 1608—Alex' Moir, &c.; 2. Nicoll, 4th April 1613; 3. George, 6th Aug' 1615.

1607. July 5. Alexander Moir and Mariorie Marno married.
    1. Thomas, 15th March 1610; 2. A son, 11th Aug' 1611; 3. Thomas, 16th July 1613; 4. A son, 23d Feb' 1616.

1613. Nov'. Peter Moir and Elspet Croser married.
    1. Peter, 30th Sept' 1616; 2. Agnes, 26th Dec' 1618; 3. Mariorie, 1st Dec' 1628; 4. Janet, twin with last—Mr. Jas. Moir, &c.; 5. Elspet, 1st April 1630; 6. Christian, 23d Oct' 1632; 7. Margaret, twin with last.

1618. George Angus and Katherine Moir married.

1620. Sept' 11. Andrew Gray and Margaret Moir had Margaret.

1622. Feb' 21. Alexander Steinson and Margaret Moir had a daughter.

William Moir and Issobell Meassone.
    1. Samuel, 15th July 1624; 2. Alexander, 24th March 1629; 3. Patrick, 7th Sept' 1631; 4. Issobell, 28th Nov' 1635; 5. James, 14th March 1639.
William Moir and Elspet Meassone had Susanna, 3d Nov' 1637.

1628. July 24. Ronald Moir and Agnes Cargill had William.

Mr. William Moir and Janet Forbes.
    1. Bessie, 28th Oct' 1641; 2. Andrew, 31st Aug' 1643.

1628. Mr. William Moir and Jean Forbes married 10th Aug', designed 1639, &c. baillie (was elected to the Town Council of Aberdeen 1595-6, or at least a Mr. William Moir was), Principal of Marischal College, and his widow, Jean Forbes, is alive, and polled in 1696. Kennedy's Annals, p. 223. Poll-Book, vol. ii., p. 624.
    1. Agnes, 27th May 1629; 2. Jean, 29th June 1630; 3. Andrew, 2d Sept' 1631; 4. John, 16th Nov' 1632; 5. Jeane, 17th June 1634 (see p. 87); 6. Patrick, 10th March 1638; 7. Issobell, 3d Dec' 1639; 8. Elizabeth, 13th Oct' 1648—John More, a godfather.

1629. May 9. Jo. Gray and Margaret Moir had William.

1629. June 14. John Robertson and Agnes Moir married.

1630. Jany 3. Joⁿ Knowlly and Margaret Moir had Janet.

> A family named Knowles owned the property of Logie-
> rieve, in the parish of Udny, in the end of the sixteenth
> century.

1633. Joⁿ Moir and Christian Kinnaird married.

> Robert Gray and Agnes Moir.
>> 1. Robert, 23d July 1630; 2. Agnes, 1st Novr 1631;
>> 3. Margaret, 30th March 1633; 4. Jean, 30th
>> April 1635.

1633. Thomas Moir and Jean Lamb married 3d Jan^y.
>> 1. Walter, 14th Novr 1633—Mr. Walter Moir, a god-
>> father; 2. Patrick, 30th April 1635; 3. Elspet, 8th
>> Feby 1638; 4. John, 21st Octr 1640; 5. Jean, 6th
>> April 1643.

1634. Mr. James Moir and Marione Edie married 2d Dec^r.

> She had probably been an Aedie of Newark, pp. 53, 65.

1636. June 11. Mr. William Moir and Elspet Forbes had Alexander.

1639. Augt 11. Gilbert Moir and Margaret Ferguson had Jean.

1638. June 19. Robert Cruickshank and Margaret Moir married.

1645. April 11. Umquhill Gilbert Moir and Janet Clark had
Hector bap.

1637. Novr 21. George Moir and Issobell Rickart married.
>> 1. Christina, 1st Septr 1639—Pat^k Moir, a godfather; 2.
>> William, 1st April 1641—Mr. Wm. Moir, &c.; 3.
>> Agnes, 18th Jany 1652—John More, &c., god-
>> fathers.

1640. Novr 30. George Dewgeth (Duguid) and Grisell Moir had
John.

1641. Decr 21. Andrew Moir and Annas Lumsden married,

> Adam Moir and Christian Forbes.
>> 1. William, 8th April 1642—Wm. Moir, Bailzie, and Pat^k
>> Moir, godfathers; 2. John, 26th April 1649; 3.
>> Margaret, 1st July 1651—Robert Moir, &c.

Andrew More and Barbara Boyes.
    1. Elspet, 29th Oct' 1654—Alex' More, &c.; 2. George,
    11th Sept' 1656—Geo. Boyes, &c.

1641. July 27. James Rob and Janet Moir married.
    1. James, 24th April 1642.

1643. Feb'y 9. James Moir and Christian Selbie married.

1644. June 18. Jo⁰ Moir and Agnes Spinola married.

1647. April 20. Thomas More and Janet Coupper married.
    1. Barbara, 30th Jan'y 1648.

1647. Feb'y 9. Jo⁰ Moir and Margaret Purò married.

John More and Issobell Findlay.
    1. John, 31st Oct' 1648.

Robert More and Margaret Pressie (Presley).
    1. Janet—John More, a godfather.

1648. Nov' 21. John More and Janet Johnstoune married.
    1. Alexander, 24th Sept' 1649—Alex' More, a god-
    father.

Patrick Gellie of Balgerso and Margaret More.
    1. Wm., 24th Sept' 1648—Wm. More, elder and y', &c.,
    godfathers; 2. Alex', 11th Aug' 1650—Alex' Jaffray,
    Provost, John Jaffray, Baillie; 3. Robert, 18th May
    1652; 4. Paull, 15th Jan'y 1654; 5. James, 8th
    Nov' 1655; 6. Issobell, 12th Oct' 1660.

The Gellies, who were considerable merchants at Aberdeen, owned, for some generations, the estate of Blackford,
in Aberdeenshire, and seemed to have several times intermarried with the Moirs and Byres families.

Alexander Gellie [1] of Blackford, 1672-8, bears argent
an ark in the waters proper, surmounted of a dove azure,
bearing in her beak an olive branch vert.

1670. April 15.—" Patrick Gellie,[2] heir of Patrick Gellie,
merchant burgess of Aberdeen, his father, in the lands of
Balgerso, parish of Foveran."—*Retours*.

Alexander More Baxter and Janet Runsieman.
    1. Bessie, 25th April 1650; 2. Janet, 13th Oct' 1653.—

---

[1] Appears with his wife and family as alive 1695-6.

[2] Appears in same record, designed " late baillie."

Poll-Book. vo'.
ii., p. 598.
Ibid., p. 606.

Pat^k More, Bailie, &c.; 3. Alexander, 24th April 1656.

1652. Mr. John Campbell married Jean Moir, dau. of Mr. William Moir, Principal, and Jean Forbes, p. 85, 14th June.

    1. Wm., 20th March 1654—Mr. Wm. Moir, Principal, Pat^k Moir, Bailey; 2. Elizabeth, 20th May 1658—Wm. Moir, Principal, and Wm. Moir, godfathers; 3. James, 30th Decr 1659; 4. John, 12th June 1662; 5. Robt, 28th June 1663; 6. Janet, 19th Augt 1665; 7. Patrick, 14th Jany 1667; 8. Margaret, 16th March 1668; 9. George, 16th Augt 1669; 10. Margaret, 21st Septr 1670; 11. Anna, 11th July 1674.

1654. Octr 1. William Smith and Edrine More, in Oldtown parish, dau. Janet.

1654. Dec^t31. Gilbert Davidson and Margaret More have Matthew bap.—Dr. Wm. More, &c. godfathers.

1655, March 27. John More and Agnes More, Oldtown, Barbara, bap.

1655. Alexander Burnett, designed "Polls," and Agnes Moir married June 26.

    1. Margaret, 20th Augt 1657—Alex^r Burnet, late Bailie, Pat^k Moir, &c. godfathers; 2. Thomas, 16th Jany 1659; 3. Geils, 19th Feby 1661—Mr. Robt Burnet of Colpnay, &c.; 4. Agnes, 15th March 1663—John Jaffray, late Provost, &c.; 5. Alexander, 2d Feby 1665; 6. Marjorie, 14th Augt 1669 (see p. 95); 7. Robert, 7th March 1672; 8. John, 24th April 1673; 9. John, 15th Augt 1674; 10. David, 14th March 1676; 11. George, 21st Augt 1677—Geo. Skene of Fintray, Provost, Mr. Geo. Peacock, &c. godfathers; 12. Andrew, 8th Jany 1679—Wm. Cuming of Auchry, &c., godfathers; 13. Patrick, 7th Novr 1680— Pat^k Moire and Pat^k Gellie, &c.

These Burnetts were cadets of the Leys family, and Alexander Burnett, b. 1665, was first of the Burnetts of Kirkhill, now represented by the Bannermans of Elsick.

1657. June 15. William Moir and Issobell Gillanders married.

John Brannes (Brands) and Janet Moir.

 1. Agnes, 29th March 1655—Rob¹ and Geo. More, godfathers ; 2. Margaret, 22d Dec' 1658—Jo" Moir, &c.; 3. Johnne, 12th June 1662.

Thomas Mitchell and Mariorie Moir.

 1. Mariorie, 12th July 1665—Mr. Wm. Moir, Principal, Dr. Wm. Moir and John More, godfathers ; 2. Alexander, 28th Oct' 1656 ; 3. Janet, 24th Dec' 1657 ; 4. Thomas, 16th Jan'ʸ 1659 ; 5. John, 15th July 1662 ; 6. Andrew, 20th Sept' 1663 ; 7. William, 13th Sept' 1664.

Thomas Mitchell, a Bailie of Aberdeen, whose son Thomas, b. 1659, was sometime Provost of Aberdeen, and first of the Mitchells of Thainstone, see p. 19.

1655. Nov' 6. Patrick Moir and Issobell Keine, Oldtown, dau. Christian bap.

John Moir and Margaret Cruickshank (perhaps a dau. of Robert Cruickshank of Banchory, Provost of Aberdeen 1693-8).

 1. George, 5th Dec' 1661 ; 2. Jean, 9th Dec' 1662 ; 3. Margaret, 1st Jan'ʸ 1665 ; 4. John, 8th Nov' 1666 ; 5. Alex', 12th May 1668 ; 6. Margaret, 16th Feb'ʸ 1671 ; 7. James, 11th June 1673 ; 8. William.

1663. George Moiresone, Litster, and Marione Moir married, Aug' 4.

 1. George, 12th May 1663 ; 2. Robert, 28th April 1665 ; 3. John, 27th Aug' 1667.

1663. June 16. James Brown and Jean Moir married.

George Moir and Margaret Smellie married 14th July 1663.

 1. James, 5th July 1676—Jas. Moir, in Ferriehill, Jas. Carnegie, &c.; 2. Issobell, 17th May 1664.

1664. May 31. John Moir and Janet Barnet married.

1668. April 16. Walter Stewart, Merchant, Banff (Provost 1692-95) and Janet Moir married.

John Moir and Bessie Collison married 4th July 1667.

 1. Margaret, 26th Oct' 1668 ; 2. John, 3d Nov' 1670- -

John Moir of Stainiewood, John Moire of Barnes, John Moir, son to Bailie Pat^k Moir, &c. godfathers; 3. Alex^r, 21st Septr 1672; 4. Wm., 15th Novr 1673; 5. Jean, 9th March 1675; 6. George, 17th March 1677; 7. Thomas, 27th Octr 1678.

1669. April 22. Robert Moir, Litster, and Marie Paton married.

1668. Decr 8. Peter Symmer and Mariorie Moir married.

1668. Decr 12. James Schand, Cordiner, and Jean Moir married.
    1. Jean, 8th Jany 1670; 2. James, 8th April 1672; 3. Thomas, 30th April 1673; 4. Robert, 5th April 1674; 5. Janet, 23d April 1676; 6. Elizabeth, 8th Decr 1678.

1659. June 2. Andrew Moir and Jean Mackie married.
    1. Marjorie, 16th March 1660—Alex^r Moir, elder and y^r, godfathers; 2. Wm., 29th June 1667—Dr. Wm. Moir, Wm. Brannes, &c. godfathers; 3. Elizabeth, 8th Decr 1678.

1670. July 30. Andrew Moir and Hellene Ker married.
    1. Alex^r, 8th Septr 1671—Alexander Alex^r, Bailie, Alex^r Burnet, "Buchans, &c.;" 2. Anna, 3d Septr 1672 —Wm. Ker, y^r, &c.

1671. July 24. Johne Simmer and Jean Moir married.
    1. Issobell, 5th Augt 1671.

1671. April 27. Alex^r Hardie and Bessie Moir married.
    1. John, 2d Septr 1672—John Moir of Wattertoun, John Anderson, &c.; 2. Jean, 25th Decr 1673; 3. James, 10th Octr 1675; 4. Jean, 1st Decr 1677.

1674. Augt 13. Robert Weir and Issobell Moir married.
    1. John, 1st Augt 1675; 2. Issobell, 4th March 1677— Dr. Wm. Moir, Pat^k Moir, &c.; 3. Patrick, 10th Novr 1678—Pat^k Moire, Bailie, Pat^k Sibbald, Pat^k Sandilands, Pat^k Gellie, godfathers; 4. Margaret, 23d Novr 1679—David Aedie, Bailie, &c.; 5. Robert, 20th March 1681—Robt Patrie of Portlethan, &c.; 6. Anna, 26th Septr 1689; 7. Wm., 4th Augt 1682; 8. Walter, 26th Augt 1683—Walter Stewart, Provost of Banff, &c.; 9. Jean, 1st Jany 1688—John Moire, Bailie, &c.; 10. Wm. 5th May 1689—Dr. Wm. Moir, Wm. Souper, Wm. Black, &c.

1679. Donald Riach, weaver, and Christian Moir, married 18th
Dec^r.

    1. Issobell, 19th Decr 1680; 2. Christian, 18th Dec^r
1681; 3. Janet, 22d June 1684; 4. Margaret,
20th Septr 1685; 5. Christian, 10th April 1692—
Alex^r Strachan of Clerkseat, &c.; 6. Patrick,
17th March 1695—Patrick Gelly, &c.

1680. June 20. William Moir and Jean Clerk married.

1680. Archibald Campbell and Jean Moir married 23d Nov^r.

    1. Issobell, 29th Jan^r 1682—Pat^k Moir, Bailie, Dr. Wm.
Moir, &c.

1681. Augt 30. Robert Moir and Elspet Moir married.

    John Moir, merchant burgess of Aberdeen, designed
1684 "late theasurer"; 1687 Bailie, deceased 1699,
married Jean Campbell 29th April 1683.

    1. Pat^k 23d Decr 1683—Mr. Pat^k Sandilands of Cotton,
Dr. Pat^k Chalmer, &c.; 2. John, 7th Decr 1684—
John Leslie of Colpnay, John Souper, &c.; 3.
Jean, April 4, 1686—Wm. More, Geo. Leslie,
Provost, Gilbert Black, Bailie, &c.; 4. Wm. 8th
Novr 1687—Dr. Wm. More, Wm. Souper; 5. Issobell,
10th Octr 1688—Sir Thos. Burnet, &c.; 6. Elspet,
25th June 1690—And^w Fraser, Sherif-Depute, &c.;
7. Margaret, 2d Septr 1691; 8. John, 13th Nov^r
1692—Mr John Campbell, y^r, writer to ther ma.
signet, John Johnston of Newplace, &c.; 9.
Gilbert, 15th Decr 1693 — Gilbert Moir, eldest
lawful son to the late Mr. Wm. Moir, Dr. in Physick;
10. Patrick, 12th Octr 1695—Mr. Pat^k Chalmers,
Dr. of Medicine, &c.; 11. James, 24th March 1698
—Mr. Jas. Moir, Regent; 12. Issobell (posthumous
child), 22d Decr 1699—Thos. Mitchell, Lord
Provost, presenter of child in place of deceased
father.

1684. Decr 18. John Black, smyth, and Janet Moir, married.

1683. William Moir, messenger, and Christian Ray, married 14th
June.

    1. Katherine, 29th June 1684—John Moir, theasurer,
John Moir, merchand, Geo. Keith, &c., godfathers; 2. John, 2d May 1686—John More,

theasurer, John More in Gellen or Ellon, Mr.
John More, Stanniwood's brother, John More,
merchand, John More, student, &c.

1683. Oct' 16. George Moir, miller, and Christian Craigheid,
married.

1698. May 30. Alexander Moir and Jean Burnett married.
Alexander Moir, younger, and Janet Currie.
 1. Andrew, 23d April 1657; 2. Janet, 13th May 1658;
 3. Elspet, 12th May 1660; 4. Alexander, 29th
 June 1662; 5. Margaret, 23d July 1663; 6. John,
 11th March 1666—John Moir of Barnes and John
 Moir, y', godfathers; 7. Agnes, 26th Nov' 1668; 8.
 Issobell, 6th Oct' 1672; 9. Alexander, 19th Oct'
 1673; 10. James, 7th Feb'' 1675; 11. Margaret,
 2d July 1676; 12. Issobell, 24th Feb'' 1678—
 Alex' Burnett, "Buchans," Pat' Strinach, &c., godfathers.

William Moir and Margaret Burnett.
 1. Andrew, 9th June 1657.

Andrew Moir and Janet Currie.
 1. Marjorie, 10th June 1670.

John More and Margaret Paterson.
 1. Janet, 26th Oct' 1660—Alex', Rob', and John More,
 godfathers; 2. Margaret, 15th Feb'' 1663; 3. John,
 3d Sept' 1665; 4. Robert, 2d Jan'' 1668—Pat'
 Moire, late Bailie, John Moire of Barnes, and John
 Moire, y'.

Alexander Moir or Mure and Elspet Cook.
 1. Bessie, 13th Jan'' 1661; 2. Issobell, 31st July 1662;
 3. Barbara, 2d Dec' 1664—John Souper, &c.; 4.
 Margaret, 3d Feb'' 1667; 5. Matthew, 23d April
 1669.

James Brown and Jean Moir.
 1. Bessie, 6th Feb'' 1666; 2. John, 25th Sept' 1668.

Alexander Moir and Janet or Jean Gellie.
 1. Jean, 2d June 1691—Pat' Gellie, &c.; 2. Thomas,
 19th April 1684.

John Moire and Agnes Moire.
 1. Jean, 22d Nov' 1673.

John Murray and Issobell Moire.
1. Jean, 19th April 1674—Jas. Moire, Alex' Alexander,
&c.; 2. Alexander, 20th Oct' 1676—Alex' Moire,
&c.

Patrick Moir and Janet Tortree.
1. James, 27th April 1674.

George Moir and Janet Jaffray.
1. Issobell, 10th Nov' 1674—John Moire, &c.; 2.
Issobell, 3d Sept' 1676—John Moire, Pat^k Moire,
late Bailie, &c.; 3. John, 4th May 1678; 4. Robert,
14th March 1680; 5. George, 23d April 1681.

Patrick Walker and Issobell Moir.
1. Alexander, 16th Feb' 1675; 2. George, 23d Dec'
1679.

Adam Smith and Elspet Moir.
1. Patrick, 16th May 1675—Pat^k Moire, Pat^k Gellie, &c.

Andrew Young and Janet Moir.
1. William, 10th March 1676; 2. Christian, 3d Aug^t
1678; 3. George, 9th Feb' 1680; 4. Nathaniell,
7th Feb' 1682.

William Moir, merchant, and Mariorie, dau. of late James
Walker, merchant, married.
1. James, 30th March 1686.

William Moir, elder, merchant, and Margaret, dau. of
Gilbert Black, late Bailie, married 16th June 1705.

John Moir, merchant, and Margaret Moir, dau. of the late
Baillie John Moir, married 14th Feb' 1717.

George Simson, merchant, and Jean, dau. of Gilbert Moir,
cooper, married 21st March 1719.

Alexander Moir and Jean Selbie.
1. Wm., 28th April 1678; 2. Jean, 21st Augt 1681—
Thos. Mitchell, litser, John Moire, &c.

George Largg and Margaret Moir.
1. Margaret, 8th March 1679—Geo. Moire, a godfather.

James Smith and Bessie Moire.
1. Elspet, 20th July 1679—John Moire, surgeon, &c.;
2. Christian, 25th Oct' 1681; 3. Agnes, 6th Oct'
1682; 4. George, 7th Oct' 1683; 5. Margaret, 27th
Feb' 1686.

James Robertson and Marie Moire.
 1. Jannet, 9th May 1680—Thos. Mitchell, late Bailie,
   Walter Robertson, &c.; 2. Margaret, 15th Sept' 1683
   —Mr Geo. Seaton, &c.; 3. Issobell, 26th Nov' 1685.

William Moir and Janet Beidie.
 1. Jean, 30th Sept' 1681 — John Moir, Dr. Jas. Leslie,
   Alex' King, and John Anderson ; 2. Christian,
   13th March 1687—John More, mer', &c.

John Thomson and Mariorie Mores had—
 1. Thomas, 6th Nov' 1681.

William Welch and Issobell Moir had—
 1. James, 19th Feb' 1684.

Alexander Aberdeen[1] and Margaret Moir.
 1. Issobell, 2d Aug' 1685—Sir Geo. Skene of Fintray,
   John Moir, Theasurer, John Ross, &c.; 2. A dau.,
   15th Sept' 1688—John Moir, present Bailie, and
   Robert Weir, merchant.

1687. Aug' 21. Mr. Thomas Jaffray,[2] of Dilspro, and Issobell Moir
   married.
    1. Marie, 21st Aug' 1687—Sir Geo. Skene of Fintray,
     John More, Bailie, Dr. Wm. Moir and Gilbert
     Black, late Bailie ; 2. John, 10th March 1689—
     John Moir, late Bailie, John Jaffray, son to the
     deceast David Jaffray, merchant, &c. ; 3. John,
     25th May 1690—John Sandilands, present Bailie,
     Cap' John Campbell of Moy, &c. ; 4. Margaret,
     13th Oct' 1691—Wm. Farquharson of Invercauld,
     Mr Geo. Chalmer, Rector of Foord, &c.

William Chesser, " fermer," and Helen Moir.
 1. John, 4th March 1693 ; 2. William, 10th Feb' 1695 ;
   3. James, 11th April 1697—Jas. Syper ; 4. Margaret,
   19th May 1702.

"Mr." Alexander Moir, "writer," and "messenger," also
 designed "merchant," and Anna Gordon.
 1. John, 4th June 1693—John Moir, late Bailie, John
   Moir, Town's Councillor, and John Moir, skipper,
   &c. ; 2. Alex', 24th July 1694—Mr. Alex' Moir,

[1] Dead in 1696, when his widow is polled with children, John and Issobell.
He was probably progenitor of the Aberdeins of Cairnbulg.
 [2] This was a great Quaker family, long connected with the town, and owned
for several generations the estate of Kingswells.

Regent in Marischal Coll., Alex^r Orem; 4. Wm., June
26, 1698— Wm. Moir, mer^t, brother-german to Stoneywood, Mr. Wm. Moir, messenger, Wm. Bisset, late
Dean of Gild, and Mr. Wm. Gordon, son to the
Earl of Abdⁿ, &c.; 5. A son, Septr 1699.

Alexander Moir, "burger and wright," and Marjorie
Webster.
    1. Janet, 18th March 1694— Wm. Moir, messenger;
    2. Issobell, 12th April 1696—Wm. Moir, Burges;
    3. Margaret, 28th Decr 1697.

Alexander Moir, "horsehyer," and Issobell Mathieson.
    1. Jean, 9th Septr 1689—Robt Gordon, &c.; 2. Mary,
    4th Feby 1691; 3. Mathew, 21st Decr 1692—
    Matthew M'Kaill, elder and y^r, &c.; 4. Issobell,
    24th March 1695; 5. John, 5th March 1699.

James Gordon, brother-german to the laird of Badenscoth,
and Margaret Moir.
    1. Mary, 11th May 1690—Adam Gordon of Inver-
    bucket, and John Moir, late bailie, &c.; 2.
    (blank), 6th March 1691; 3. Anne, 25th Oct^r
    1691—Alex^r Gordon, late Lord Provost, Adam
    Gordon of Inverebrie, &c.; 4. Helen, 16th Feb^y
    1693—Mr Geo. Moir, Regent, &c.; 5. Jean, 1st
    Feby 1694—John Moir, late Bailie.

George Ferguson and Elspet Moir.
    1. Janet, 9th Novr 1690—Pat^k Gellie, &c.

John Strachan, merchant, and Margaret Moir.
    1. Alex^r, 19th May 1691—Alex^r Strachan of Clerkseat,
    late Dean of Gild; 2. James, 3d July 1692; 3. Wm.
    8th Octr 1693; 4. Issobell, 16th Decr 1694; 5.
    Ann, 9th March 1697; 6. Elizabeth, 27th Dec^r
    1698.

James Moir, Regent in Marischal Coll., and Marjorie
Burnett, probably dau. of Alexander Burnett and Agnes
Moir, p. 88.
    1. Agnes, 16th April 1693—Alex^r Moir, Regent, &c.;
    2. Janet, 2d Octr 1694—Mr Thos. Burnet, advo-
    cate, and John Burnet, designed "Poles"; 3.
    Jean, 23d Augt 1695; 4. Janet, 12th Jany 1698;

5. Rachell, 11th Nov' 1699—Pat^k Gellie, late
bailie, Mr Alex' Moir, Regent, &c. ; 6. Alex', 14th
Jan' 1701—Mr Alex' Moir, Regent, and Alex' Moir
of Scotstoun, &c. ; 7. James, 31st July 1702—
Jas. Moir, of Stoneywood, Jas., son to the late
Bailie John Moir, &c. ; 8. James, April 8, 1703—
Mr Andw. Burnet, minister, and Dr. in Physick,
Thos. Burnet of Kirkhill, adv' in Edinbro', and
John Burnet, mer', "designed Poles "; 9. Jean,
19th March 1705—Jas. Moir of Stoneywood, and
Wm. Moir, mer'.

William Fettes, burges and tailour, and Anna Moir.
1. John, 12th July 1694—John Moir, tailor, &c. ; 2.
Anna, 1st Sept' 1695 — John Lesley of Colpnay,
&c. ; 3. Margaret, 29th Aug' 1699—James Davidson of Tillymorgan, &c. ; 4. James, 6th Aug' 1700.

Gilbert Moir, burges and Cooper, and Margaret Barclay.
1. Margaret, 5th May 1695—Wm. Moir, mer', Mr. Geo.
Leslie ; 2. Anna, 28th May 1699—Alex' Aberdeen, &c.

Gilbert Moir and Margaret Moir.
1. Jean, 7th March 1697.

Cap' John Anderson, mer' and skipper, and Janet Moir.
1. John, 16th Nov' 1698.

Thomas Orem, merchant, present Master of the Gild
Hospital, and Agnes Moir.
1. Margaret, 17th Aug' 1701—Mr. Thos. Orem, of
Glasgow—Alex' Orem, present Bailie ; 2. Wm., 2d
May 1703 ; 3. John, 12th Nov' 1705.

Cap' James Gordon of Barnes, and Margaret Moir (probably dau. of John Moir of Barnes and Mary Cochran,
p. 80).
1. Margaret, 12th Oct' 1701—Adam Gordon of Inver-
ebrie, adv', and Wm. Gordon of Old Govell, and
Pat^k Gordon, mer' ; 2. Issobell, 23d Oct' 1702—
Mr. Alex' Gordon, factor in Campheir, and Wm.
Gordon of Kintore ; 3. Christian, 27th April
1704 ; 4. Margaret, 7th Oct' 1705.

SURNAME OF BYRES.

Like most names, we find it spelt in a variety
of ways, Birs, Bires, Byres, de Byres, Byris, Birss,
Byrs, Byires, Byrris, Byers, Buyers, &c., and it had
no doubt been assumed from the lands of Byres, in
the parish and county of Haddington; a district
with which the progenitors of the family about to be
treated of, appear to have been for some time connected.   There is a tradition that the family of
Byres was of Hungarian origin, and settled for a
time in France, and that the direct ancestor of
Byres, of Coates, accompanied Mary of Guise,
Queen of James V., to Scotland; but I can find no
evidence of this, and as I will afterwards shew,
people of this surname held land in Edinburgh in
the 14th century.   It is worthy of remark, as shew-
ing that the descendants of the Coates family, the
Byres of Tonley, who acquired that property in
1718, had some faith in "the Guise story," as one
of the principal farms on that estate is called
Guise, although there is no such place on the
property when the Poll Book of Aberdeenshire was
made up, 1695–6.   There are also other places of
the name of Byres in Scotland, as one in the county
of Perth, another near Fochabers, in Morayshire, &c.
Mr Stodart, Lyon Depute, suggests that in some
cases, the name in Aberdeenshire may have been

N

assumed from the parish of *Birse*, in that county.
The surname is certainly occasionally written Birs,
&c. See above. There was a family named Byres,
long settled in Northamptonshire; in the time of
Edward IV., a Miss Byres marries William Kingscote, of Kingscote, in the county of Gloucester.

Byers.—" The chateau of Biars, in the canton of
Isiqui, La Manche, in Normandy, temp. Conquest,
had lords of its own name."

The family of Byres, of Coates, rose to wealth
and station as merchant burgesses of Edinburgh, and
acquired that property by purchase from the Kincaids, as will be afterwards shewn; and their *probable*
progenitors were long connected with the counties
of Midlothian, Haddington, Lanark, &c.

1392. Thomas de Byres is mentioned in the
    chartulary of St Giles, as owning lands in
    Edinburgh.

1468. Robert Birs, notary.

1469. Duncan of Birs, Aberdeenshire.

1502. John Byrs, { in Montrose, } Register of the
    mentioned in { Great Seal, vol.
    „ George Byrs, { a charter. } ii., 2716.

1565. Bernard Byre, "Ducheman"—Privy Council
    Records, vol. i., p. 429.

1590. Thomas Byris, in Ardgowan, Ayrshire.—*Ibid.*
    1623, James Byres, in Ardgowan (probably
    a son).

1585. James Byris is mentioned. Acts of Parliament
    of Scotland, vol. iii., p. 389, James VI.

1592. 2. Sept' Margaret Hunter, in Kincardine
    O'Neil, and Andrew Byres, her son, when
    Patrick Hunter, burgess of Aberdeen, is
    their cautioner for £500 each, that they will

not harm Patrick Leslie, son of James
Leslie, burgess of Aberdeen, or Janet Hunter his spouse. Privy Councell Records, vol.
v., p. 567.

1595. Geordie Byris, in Lymkills, county Dumfries.
—*Ibid.*, p. 380.

1593. 14th Nov' Thomas Byris, in Ressavit, Aberdeenshire.—*Ibid.*, 606.

Register of St Nicholas, Aberdeen.

1574. Duncan Wrytin, and Christen Byrris, married
4th July.

1. James, bap. 7th Feb' 1573. Unless
there is a mistake in the register, it
would appear this son was born out
of wedlock.

1578. Alexander Byeris, and Janet Blinschell.

1. Christion, bap. 14th Sept'·

1618. David Gray, and Margaret Byrris, a daughter
Janet, 27th June.

"BYRES CLOSE"—AND COATES HOUSE.

From Old and New Edinburgh, vol. i., p. 153.—
"Prior to the year 1811, there remained unchanged
in the Luckenbooths two lofty houses of great
strength and antiquity, one of which contained the
town residence of Sir John Byres, Bart. of Coates,
an estate now covered by the west end of New
Edinburgh. He was a gentleman who made a
great figure in the city during the reign of James
VI., but no memories of him now remain, save the
alley called Byres Close, and his tomb in the west
wall of the Greyfriars' Churchyard, the inscription on

which, though nearly obliterated, tells us that he was treasurer, baillie, and dean of guild of Edinburgh, and died in 1629, in his sixtieth year."

There are several inaccuracies in the above statement. Sir John Byres of Coates was a simple Knight, not a Baronet, and was son of John Byres I. of Coates, the Treasurer, &c., of Edinburgh, who died in 1629, in his sixtieth year, and it was to him, and not to his son Sir John Byres, that the tombstone was erected.

COATES HOUSE (CALLED EASTER COATES).

Ibid., vol. ii., pp. 115–16.—" The lands and houses of Easter and Wester Coates lay westward of Bearfold's Parks and the old Ferry Road. The former edifice, a picturesque old mansion, with turrets, dormer windows, and crow-stepped gables, in the Scoto-French style, still remains unchanged, among its changed surroundings, as when it was built—probably about 1611—by Sir John Byres, of Coates, whose town residence was in Byres Close, in the High Street, and over the door of which he inscribed the usual pious legend, 'Blissit be God in al his giftis,' with the initials of himself and his lady. This lintel was removed by the late Sir Patrick Walker, who had succeeded to the estate, and was rebuilt by him into the present ancient house, which is destined long to survive as the deanery of St Mary's Cathedral. Into the walls of the same house were built some fragments of sculpture from a mansion in the Cowgate, traditionally known as the residence of the French embassy in Mary's time. They are now in the north wing. On the eastern side of the mansion of Coates are two ancient lintels, one dated 1600 with the initials C.C.I. and K.H. ; the other bears the same initials, with the legend, 'I prays ye Lord For All His Benefetis—1601.' On the west a dormer gable bears the date 1615, with the initials—J.B.M.B., that is, John Byres, and Margaret Barclay, his first wife,—and a stone built above the western door bears in large letters the word Jehova, with the city motto, and the date 1614. Prior to the time of the Byres the property had belonged to the Lindsays, as in the ratification of Parliament to Lord Lindsay in 1592 are mentioned 'the landis of Dene, but the mylnes and mure thereof, and their pertenents lyand within the Sherifdom of Edinburgh, the manes of Drym, the lands of Drymhill, the lands of Coittis, and Coitakirs,' &c." (Acta Parl. Jacobi VI.)

1576, 22d March, the will of Johne Johnestoun of the Cottis, burgess of Edinburgh, is recorded. Perhaps he is ancestor of the Johnstons, who appear to have been related to Agnes Smyth, II. wife of John Byres I. of Coates, see p. 107. Afterwards Coates belonged to the Kincaids, who sold it to John Byres early in the 17th century. By the last family it was sold to Lord Roseberry in 1702. Sir Patrick Walker, the late owner of the estate, succeeded his father, the Rev⁴ William Walker (of Old Meldrum, Aberdeenshire), who bought the property.

JOHN BYRES, I. OF COATES.

"Rule be one."

I. John Byres, born circa 1569, I. of Coates, an eminent and leading merchant burgess (admitted 1595, see p. 147) of Edinburgh, was two years Bailie, six years Treasurer, six years, 1619–24, Dean of Guild, and two years Old Provost of the capital of Scotland.

Acts of Parliament of Scotland, vol. iv. pp. 606 and 629. Mr Byres was one of the commissioners appointed by James VI., "anent the plantation of kirks, as sit unplantit," and also in the commission by the same monarch in 1621, "anent moneyis."

Privy Council Records, vol. v. p. 764. 1597. 14th Septr. Robert Jolie, burgess of Edinburgh, "being in his voyage towards Burdeaux in France, and uncertain of his return, is not able to keep the day appointed for his compearance for the pursuit of the suspension raised by him against the Treasurer and Advocat. Wherefore there is a warrant under the sign manual, and countersigned by J. Lindesay, secretary to John Andro, to delete the act of caution whereby Jolie has found John Dougall, and John Byris, sureties for his compearance upon 11th November next.

Ibid. p. 688. 1598. 28th April. "Johnne Robertsoun younger, merchant burgess of Edinburgh, appears for Johnne Byris, merchant burgess there, to satisfy the comptroller for the custom of 30 lasts of beens, imported by him."

Ibid. p. 704. 1598. 14th Septr. At Edinburgh, "Johnne Byris, merchant burgess of Edinburgh, appears for Johnne Ros, minister at Dumbartane, to make the teind

sheaves of the parsonage of Dumbartane furthcoming
to all parties having interest." John Byres acquired
early in the 17th century, probably about 1610, by
purchase from the Kincaids, the estate of Coates, in
the parish of St. Cuthbert's, as well as other property
(see Extracts from Sasines, p. 161), on which so much
of the west end of Edinburgh is now built, and
erected the present interesting old mansion house,
likely in 1615. For an account of it see pp. 4,5.
This laird of Coates, who was a man of very considerable influence and importance, died in 1629, and
there is a very fine monument to his memory, erected
by his widow Agnes Smyth, and children, see p. 143.
By his first wife, Dame Margaret Barclay, who had
probably been of the ancient house of Barclay of
Towie, in Aberdeenshire, who died 12th Janʸ 1616,
(for a copy of her will see p. 148), he appears
to have had daughters only.

I. John Byres of Coates, and Dame Margaret
Barclay, his first wife. Issue, three daughters :—

  1. Margaret Byres, mᵈ Alexander Heriot,¹ mer-
     chant burgess of Edinburgh. Issue, six sons
     and four daughters :—
     1. Alexander, bap. 14th Novʳ 1619. Witnesses,
        Mʳ John Jolie, Dʳ of Physick, John Byres,
        and Thomas Charteris, merchants.
     2. Thomas, bap. 22d July 1621.
     3. James, bap. 19th Augᵗ 1623. Witnesses, Mʳ

¹ The Heriots, who intermarried with the Primroses (Roseberry),
and Foulis' of Ravelston, were of the same stock as George
Heriot—" Jingling Geordie "—the munificent founder of Heriot's
Hospital.

James Oliphant, advocate, and John
Kennerd, younger of Fordie, &c.

4. Robert, bap. 30th Dec' 1626. Witnesses, M'
Robert Winrame, M' Rob' Burnet,
younger, Advocate, and John Byres.

5. George, bap. 3d Jany. 1630. Witnesses, Geo.
Fowlis, M' Geo. Butler, Geo. Scott, and
Geo. Arnot.

6. David, bap. 2d March 1631. Witnesses,
David Cunninghame, of Akinhervie, M'
David Mitchell, minister, M' David
Heriot, Advocate, and M' William Scott,
D' of Physick.

1. Agnes, bap. 25th July 1622. Witnesses, John
Byres, Ja' Heriot, Litster, &c.

2. Isobel, bap. 21st Oct' 1624. Witnesses,
Johne Byris, M' David Heriot, and John
Howstoun.

3. Rachel, bap. 3d Jany. 1626. Witnesses, M'
Johne Olyphant, M' James Inglis, and
George Arnot.

4. Elizabeth, bap. 21st Dec' 1627. Witnesses,
M' John Jolie, D' of Physick, Tho' Weir,
and John Pearsone.

2. Rachel Byres, m' the Rev' Thomas Sydserff[1]
(eldest son of James Sydserff, merchant-
burgess of Edinburgh), one of the ministers

---

[1] "Thomas Sydserff, afterwards Dean of Edinburgh, was consecrated Bishop of Brechin 1634, and translated to Galloway in
the following year. At the Restoration he was the only surviving
Scottish Bishop, and died 16 ."—Stodart's "Scottish Arms,"
vol. ii., p. 132. He had no doubt been a cadet of the old family
of Sydserff of that ilk. There are still the Buchan-Sydserffs,
of Ruchlaw, in the county of Haddington.

of St. Giles, Edinburgh (M.A. 1602). Issue,
three sons and four daughters :—

1. Johnne, bap. 25th Novr 1621.
2. Thomas, bap. 8th Octr 1624, who fought
   under Montrose, and was knighted.
   Witnesses, Mr Alex^r Kincaid, D^r in
   Physick, Thos Weir, Thos Charteris,
   mercht^s, and Thos Miller.
3. Alexander, bap. 4th Decr 1625.
1. Margaret, bap. March 16. 1619. Witnesses,
   Johne Byris, bailie, Mr John Hall, minister, &c.
2. Elspet, bap. Octr 5. 1620. Witnesses, Johne
   Byris and Alex^r Heriot, &c.
3. Agnes, bap. Septr 4. 1627. Witnesses, M^r
   Johne Struthers, Mr Johne Maxwell,
   Johne Byris, and Mr Robert Burnet.
4. Marione, bap. Octr 25. 1628. Witnesses,
   David Aikinheid, Provost of Edinburgh,
   Mr Henrie Rollok, Mr David Mitchell,
   minister, Mr Robt Monteith.

3. Agnes Byres, died Augt 1631 [1] (3d dau. of
   John Byres, I. of Coates, and of his 1st
   wife Margaret Barclay), sole executrix to

Scott's Fasti, Part i. p. 8.

Edinbro' Wills.

---

[1] Will given up by her husband as administrator to her children,
who are minors, viz., John, Thos, Alex^r, Marg^t, Agnes, Rachel,
and Janet. Inventory of goods in hand, £5,650. Among the
debtors are George Viscount Dupplin, Chancelor of Scotland ;
Wm Earl of Morton, Treasurer ; John Lord Traquair, &c. ; total,
£17,383, 6s. 8d. Amongst the debts due is to Mr John Chartres,
minister at Currie, co. Edinburgh, £1260 ; Mr Henry Charteris,
his brother, £500. To the children of the late Mr Henry Chartres,
Prof. of Divinity, Edinbro, King James Coll. or University,
£1400, &c.

her mother, m^d 2. Septr 1619 Thomas
Charteris, merchant-burgess of Edinburgh,
designed 1625 " Baillie of Leyth." Issue,
four sons and four daughters :—

Edinburgh
City Parish
Registers.—
Marriages.

1. Henrie, bap. 15. Jany. 1622. Witnesses,
   Mr Henrie Charteris (Professor of Di-
   vinity, University of Edinburgh), Alex^r
   Heriot.
2. Johne, bap. 4. Dec. 1623. Witnesses, John
   Byris, &c.
3. Thomas, bap. 5. Jany. 1625. Witnesses,
   Thos Fisher, Mr Thos Sydserff, minister,
   and William Gray, merchant.
4. Alexander, bap. 8. March 1730. Witnesses,
   Mr Alexander Thomson, Alexander
   Spence, Alexander Heriot, Alexander
   Denistoun.
1. Margaret, bap. 8. Octr 1620. Witnesses,
   John Byris and Henry Charteris.
2. Agnes, bap. 11. Feby. 1626. Witnesses,
   John Byris, Mr Alex^r Kincaid, and John
   Pearsone.
3. Marione, bap. 3. April 1627. Witnesses,
   David Aikenheid, Provest, John Byris,
   Mr Robert Burnet, yor, Advocat.
4. Rachel, bap. 30. Novr 1628. Witnesses,
   Mr Jolie, Doctor in Physick, Alex^r Den-
   nistoun, John Smyth, and David Moore-
   heid, merchants. M^d Robert Brown,
   merchant, of Edinburgh, and had Janet,
   1659.

I. John Byres, I. of Coates, married 2dly, 1617–18, Agnes (who, on the death of John Byres, married Rev⁴ James Reid, of St. Cuthbert's, Edinburgh ; see note on family of Smyth, p. 179), daughter of Robert Smyth, merchant-burgess, of Edinburgh, by Agnes Purves his wife (see Extracts Sasines, p. 162), and sister, probably, of Sir John Smyth of Grotthill, and King's Cramond, Provost of Edinburgh, M.P. Issue, Edinburgh City Parish Registers. at least five if not six sons, viz. :—

1. Johnne, his heir, bap. 18. Feby. 1619. Witnesses, Alexʳ Heriot, Joⁿ Smyth, Joⁿ Johnstone. Of him again.

2. Robert, bap. 6. May 1621. Witnesses, Mʳ Catalogue of Graduates. Index of Retours, 743, xix. 79. Thoˢ Sydserff (his brother-in-law) and Robᵗ Smyth, child's grandfather, studied at Edinburgh University, M.A. July 1637, Advocate of that town, admitted 1642, served heir of conquest of his immediate younger brother "Mr Thomas" in 1647, and same year appointed tutor or guardian to his two nephews, George and John, sons of his elder brother Sir John Byres, (see p. 110), married Elizabeth Aikenhead, probably daughter of David Aikenhead, Provost of Edinburgh.

1. Marie, bap. 1. July 1643. Witnesses, Mʳ James Reid, Mʳ James Aikinhead, advocat, Sir John Smyth, Sir John Byres, Mʳ Thomas Aikinheid, Commisar, and John Ramsay.

3. Thomas, bap. 8. May 1623. Witnesses, Mr Tho' Sydserff, minister, Tho' Chartres, &c., studied at Edinburgh University, M.A. 15. July 1641, married Isabel, dau. of the late Captain John Conynghame, heir portioner of the lands of Saughtonhall, Midlothian, and died in 1647. (Copy of his will, see p. 156).

Retours.

4. Alexander, bap. 19. April 1625. Merchant-burgess,—admitted 4. Jany. 1660, see p. 148 —of Edinburgh, designed "of St. Leonards," near that town, served heir of line of his immediate elder brother " Mr Thomas," 3. Decr 1647, died in 1660; will confirmed 26. Augt 1661, married, contract dated 17. Novr 1648, Jean (who died 1674), dau. of Mr James Drummond, of St. Ninian's Chapel, by Jean Fowler his spouse. (This lady had two brothers, Robert and Patrick, and a sister, Jean Drummond.) In 1643, Alexander Byres has, along with his brothers Mr Robert and Mr Thomas, a charter of part of the land of St. Leonards (see Extracts from Sasines p. 165).

1. Alexander, II. of St. Leonards, bap. 15. July 1660,[1] married Margaret Tarbat, and in 1709 Anne Byres is served heir general of her mother, and in the following year of her father.

---

[1] 1685. 18. Nover. Alex^r Byirs, po^r of St Lenord's, and Mar^t Torbit, a daughter named Anna. Witnesses, James Douglas, and James Torbit. The child baptised by a line from Mr Trotter, of their lawfull marriage of this dait.

1. Jean, bap. 13. Septr 1649. Witnesses, M^r
Ja^s Reid, Mr Robt Byres, John Stirling,
&c.

2. Helen, born 1657,[1] married James Tarbat, Edinburgh
City Parish
merchant-burgess, of Edinburgh, both Registers.
alive 1661.

3. Agnes, bap. 24. April 1651. Witnesses, John
Pearsone, mert., Johne Stirling, of Baler-
no, and Ludovick Maitland, gentleman.

5. William (5th son of John Byres, I. of Coates,
and Agnes Smyth), bap. 13. April 1627.
Witnesses, Mr William Struthers, Mr William
Arthoure, and Robt Burnett, Advocat.

6. James, who must have been born 1628–30.
(John Byres, *his reputed father*, having died
in Novr 1629), merchant of Aberdeen—see
p. 114—ancestor of Byres of Tonley. In the
pedigree before quoted, this James is called
" son of James Byres, younger brother of
Sir John Byres of Coates, who served under
the Marquis of Montrose, and was slain
fighting under his command at the battle of
the Bridge of Dee, near Aberdeen, in 1644,"
&c. I have, however, found this pedigree,
written about 1773, so very incorrect and
unreliable, that I am inclined to think the
doughty Captain James Byres a mythical
personage. For the present I am not sorry
to say farewell to this warrior, who I hope, *if
he ever existed*, caused the gallant Montrose
much less trouble and thought, than he has
occasioned the writer of this family history.

[1] 1657. 2. July. Alexander Byars, Jean Durmond, a daughter
Helline. Witnesses, Mr James Reid, Johne Byres of Coats.

SIR JOHN BYRES, II. OF COATES.

II. Sir John Byres, II. of Coates, and I. of
Warrestone, born as before stated in Feby. 1619;
educated at the University of Edinburgh, M.A. 25.
July 1635; served heir to his father in the lands of
Coates, &c., by precept of Clare, 2d Nov[r] 1630; in
Sasine termed "a discreet young man," see p. 164.
Sir John Byres, who acquired the estate of Warres-
tone, county Edinburgh, was a devoted loyalist, and
engaged in the civil wars of that period. He was
knighted for his services between the years 1640-3,
see p. 165, and was shortly afterwards imprisoned at
S[t] Andrews. Warrand (see p. 143).

Sir John, who "made a great figure" in the city and
neighbourhood of Edinburgh, see p. 99, married
Isobel Auchmuty, doubtless a daughter of Sir John
Auchmuty of Gosford, descended of the old family of
Auchmuty of that ilk,[1] in the parish of Markinch, and
county of Fife, and was dead in 1648, when his will is
recorded. Copy—see p. 154.

Issue, at least three sons, viz. :—

Retours.

1. George, both alive, and minors, in 1648, when
2. John,   their uncle "Maister Robert Byres,
born 1639.[2] advocate," is appointed their tutor or
  guardian. George must have died
  young. Of John again, as heir.

---

[1] Auchmuty of that ilk bears argent two spur-rowels in chief,
and a spear head in base, azure. Sir John Auchmuty of Gosford,
East Lothian, of this family, was keeper of the wardrobe to Charles I.

St. Cuthbert's
Edinburgh.
Reg. of Bap.
1573-1700.

[2] 1639. 3. Sep[r] Mr Johne Byres of Coittis. W., Auchinmutie,
a son Johne. W., erle Lawderdaill, Sir John Auchinmutie of
Gosfard, Williame, Master of Gray.

3. Thomas, bap. 29. April 1647. Witnesses, Sir
William Gray, see p. 179; Mr Thomas
Byres (child's uncle); and Mr James Reid,
minister, see p. 107. At this time the
family appears to have been very prosperous. There is a picture of Sir John
Byres, by Jamesone, at Tonley.

"1632, 30. Jan^y, Mr Johne Byres, of Cotts,
is a witness to the baptism of John, son
to William Fairlie, of Bruntsfield, and
Margaret Skeene."

"1642, July 10, Sir John Byres, and M^r
Robert Byres, are witnesses to the baptism
of William (their brother by half blood), son
of Mr James Reid, minister, and Agnes
Smyth, the relict of John Byres, I. of Coates.

Edinburgh City Parish Registers. Register blank 1st March 1645, to 22d Jan. 1646.

JOHN BYRES, III. OF COATES.

III. John Byres,[1] of Coates, born 1639, described in genealogy before referred to as " a man of parts, but much addicted to gallantry and pleasure, and having an expensive turn, spent his estate," &c. He had not been like his father, the gallant Sir John, " a discreet young man."

Sasines.

This laird had an annuity out of the lands of Ruthven, in Inverness-shire. 12. May 1676, he married first, Jean Foulis (a daughter of the family of Foulis, Baronets of Ravelstoun and Colinton, Midlothian), probably the Jean Foulis, bap. 16. Jany. 1637, dau. of George Foulis of Ravelstoun, and Jean, dau. of Sir John Sinclair. Arms of Foulis : Argent, three laurel leaves slipped, proper.

1. George, bap. 30. Oct[r] 1659. Witnesses, George Foulis of Ravelstoun; M[r] James Reid, Minister at St Cuthbert's Kirk; M[r] John Foulis; and John Stuart, merchant.

John Byres married 2[dly], (contract, copy of, see p. 144, dated at Cupar-of-Fife 26. May 1666), Lilias, eldest daughter of Sir John Grant of that ilk, and Freuchie (progenitor of the Earls of Seafield), by Mary, daughter of Walter Lord Ogilvie of Deskford, and by her is believed to have had at least

[1] This laird is said to have left " a natural son, John Byres, who was bred to business by his relative, Robert Byres of Dublin ; after whose death, John Byres, about the year 1720, went to the East Indies, and at Fort St. George married a Portuguese lady, by whom he got a fortune, and had by her a son, John Byres, who inherited his fortune, and was lately at London," 1773.

one daughter. 1. Mary, who died unmarried, having lived latterly with her aunt, the Marchioness of Huntly; she made her will 2d May 1734, recorded _{Wills.} 16th April 1740; in it she makes her cousin-german, Anne Byres, relict of . . . Anderson, merchant, Edinburgh, her sole heir and executor, "for the love and affection she bears her." She had an annuity, dated 9th Octr 1702, of £20 sterling yearly, from Archibald, Viscount Roseberry, out of the lands of Coates, in which year that property was sold to the Primroses.

1691. June 7, John Byres of Cotts, witness to a ^{Sheriff Court Records.} service in Aberdeenshire.

At the end of this account of the family of Byres of Coates, I subjoin some extracts, no doubt referring to members of that family. ^{Edinburgh City Parish Registers.}

1633. 5. June, Mr John Pringle, and Jonat Byres, married.

1638. . . . . Robert Dowglas, husbandman, and Margaret Byres, married. ^{St. Cuthbert's}

1685. 30. July, Proclaimed, John Byres, in this ^{Parish Register— Marriages. Commence 1655. Searched to 1700.} parish, and Elspeth Gib, pledged 3 leg. dollars. Returned one-half to the said John, and the other half to the poor.

1694. 16. August, James Byres and Janet Kilpatrick were married.[1]

---

[1] The two last couples, as well as several other heads of families of the surname of Byres, appear in the St Cuthbert's register as having children baptised, but, unless remotely, they are not connected with the Coates family. I do not insert them.

P

114

II. JAMES BYRES OF ABERDEEN.

St. Nicholas's Reg. Abdn.

II. James Byres (*presumed younger son* of John Byres, I. of Coates, and Agnes Smyth—see p. 109) was married at Aberdeen 16. July 1667, to Janet Middleton,[1] stated to be a daughter of Middleton of Stenhouse. She was born circa 1637, and died at Aberdeen 25. Nov' 1695, and is interred in St. Nicholas Churchyard there. Copy of inscription on tombstone, see p. 143.

Poll Book of Aberdeenshire, vol. ii. p. 624.

"Janat Middleton, relect of James Byres, merchant, stock above 10,000 merks. Her son, Robert, 6/," servants, &c., appear as polled at Aberdeen.

Family Memoir.

Mr. Byres died at Rotterdam (before 18. April 1693), where he had gone on his business, and is buried in the Scotch kirk there. Issue, three sons and three daughters:—

Family Memoir.

1. James, bap. be M' George Meldrum, 4. March 1673 (designed in 1693, writer in Aberdeen). Ja' Lorimer, Ja' Smith, elder, Ja' Carnegie, Ja' Bartler, godfathers. Merchant burgess of Edinburgh—admitted 1695—a man of genius and enterprise. "He was the chief projector and great promoter of

---

[1] The surname of Middleton is derived from the lands of Middleton, in the county of Kincardine. Sir George Mackenzie, a contemporary of both the Earls of Middleton, says, Middleton beareth parti per fesse, or, and gules, a lion rampant, counter charged of one and the other. Towards the close of the 17th century, this family owned considerable property in Aberdeenshire, and were Principals of the University, Lairds of Seaton, near Old Aberdeen, Sheils, &c.

the Scots Expedition to Darien, and on
that account was commonly known by the
appellation of 'King of Darien.' He lost
his life and fortune in that expedition, being
killed by a French privateer in his passage
home from Lisbon, on board the packet
. .' The failure of the Darien Scheme,
through the influence of the Dutch East
India Company with William III., brought
numerous families in Scotland to ruin, made
the existing government very unpopular,
and was a great means of fomenting the
rebellion of 1715." Mr. Byres married
. . . . . , dau. of . . . . . Gellie, baillie of
Aberdeen, see p. 87, and left an only son,
who died an infant.

2. Robert, bap. 5. May 1675, be Mr Patrick
Sibbald. Godfathers, Robert Forbes, Robert Skein, elder, Robert Cruickshank,
thesaurer, Robert Innes. Of him again.

3. George, bap. 26. Jany. 1729, by last. Godfathers, Mr George Meldrum, George Rosse,
George Cruickshank, younger, George Ross,
younger, George Willocks. He settled at
Venice, where he died unmarried.

1. Jean (eldest dau. of James Byres II. and
Janet Middleton), bap. 13. Octr 1668, be M^r
Patrick Sibbald. William Gray, George
Middletoun, James Lorimer, and Andrew
Burnett of Kirkhill, witnesses. Married,
28. April 1685, William Souper of Gilcom-
ston, merchant-burgess of Aberdeen (son of
John Souper, merchant-burgess of the said
town, and of Margaret Clark). She died

[margin:] Burke's Landed Gentry, ed. 1848, Art. Farquharson of White-house.

[margin:] Memoir.

3d Jany. 1756. They appear to have had
a large family, of whom (William Souper is
designed " Master of Mortifications," 1689,
and '' Master of Kirkwork," 1693)—

WILLIAM SOUPER, OF GILCOMSTON, AND JEAN BYRES.[1]

1. John Souper, bap. 25. May 1687. John More,
   bailie, Jo^n Pirie, &c., godfathers.
2. James Souper, bap. 13. July 1689. James
   Byres, James Carnegie, godfathers.
3. William Souper, bap. 13. Octr 1691.
4. Robert Souper, bap. 5. Feby. 1695. Robert
   Byres, mer^t, &c., godfather.
5. Patrick Souper, b. 1703, died 8. Octr 1774, of
   Auchlunies, in Kincardineshire, who by his
   wife, Anne Ross, had a dau., Margaret

   Souper, married 1756, William Farquharson, M.D.; their son was the late Patrick
   Farquharson, J.P. of Whitehouse, Aberdeenshire.

1. Janet Souper, bap. 24. Feby. 1686. Pat^k
   Dovertie, bailie; Walter Robertson, dean
   of gild; Wm Livingstone, collector, &c.,
   godfathers.
2. Margaret Souper, bap. 4. Augt 1688.

---

[1] 1708. Septr 25. Wm Souper, mert., and Jean Byres his Sp.
   James, bap^t. James Catanch, Dr James Gregory, &c.
1709. Octr 25. Same couple. Thomas, bapt. Thos Mitchell
   late Provest, &c. Wit^s.
1711. July 31. Do. do. Alexander.

3. Jean Souper, bap. 6. March 1693. Geo. Keith of Crichie, &c., godfathers.
4. Isobell Souper, bap. 20. Feby. 1698. Alexr Forbes of Craigie, present bailie, and John Anderson, merchant and skipper, godfathers.

There are still people of this rather singular surname in Aberdeen. William Souper, probably of this family, of the Hon. E. I. Co.'s Service, married in 1800, Harriet Dempster, heiress of Dunnichen in Forfarshire, and Skibo in Sutherlandshire, and assumed the surname and arms of Dempster.

Ibid. Ait. Dempster.

GORDONS OF HALLHEAD AND ESSLEMONT.

2. Isabel Byres (2d dau. of James Byres II. and Janet Middleton), bap. 12. May 1670, be Mr Geo. Meldrum. Jas Webster, Alexr Walker, Gilbert Leslie, &c., godfathers. Married Robert Gordon of Aberdeen, merchant, treasurer of that town in 1688. He was afterwards a wine merchant at Bordeaux, where he amassed a considerable fortune, and was not only able to buy from his nephew, Patrick Gordon XII. of Hallhead, the old family property, which, through that laird's extravagance, would otherwise have had to pass out of the family, but also, in 1728, the ancient barony of Esslemont, in the parish of Ellon.

Registers of St. Nicholas, Aberdeen; and Pedigree, Gordon of Hallhead.

Robert Gordon XIII. of Hallhead, and I. of Esslemont, had by Isabel Byres—

1. George Gordon, XIV. of Hallhead, &c., who
   warmly espoused the cause of Charles Stuart,
   and was out in the "45," married Amy
   Bowdler; their descendant and eventual
   heiress, Anne Gordon, dau. of Robert
   Gordon of Hallhead, &c., married 1856,
   Henry Wolrige-Gordon, J.P. and D.L.,
   now of Hallhead and Esslemont, and has
   issue.

2. James Gordon, bap. 18. April 1693. Mr James
   Moir, Regent in Mareschal Coll., and James
   Byres, writer, son to the deceased James
   Byres, mer^t, godfathers.

3. Alexander Gordon, married Jane Grierson, and
   had issue.

1. Janet Gordon, bap. 24. Augt 1690. John
   Gordon, factor in Campveir, and collectors
   of their Majesties' Customs, &c., godfathers.

2. Margaret Gordon, bap. 31. Jany. 1692. David
   Aedie of New-work, &c., godfathers.

3. Isobell Gordon, 21. April 1694. Wm Souper
   of Gilcomston, Patrick Gellie, &c., godfathers.

4. Jean Gordon, bap. 9. June 1695.

5. Jean Gordon, bap. 21 Decr 1710.

Of the daughters of Robert Gordon XIII. of
Hallhead, and Isabel Byres, one married . . . .
Russell, Professor of Natural Philosophy, University
of Edinburgh ; and another married John Black of
Bordeaux, merchant, and had Dr John Black, the
celebrated chemist ; and Isobel Black, who married
James Burnett of Aberdeen, merchant, see p 181.
Their daughter, Margaret Burnett, became in 1770

the wife of her relation, Robert Byres of Kincraigie
and Memel, see p. 124.

The Byres' of Tonley are thus lineal descendants
of Robert Gordon and Isabel Byres, *aunt of* Patrick
Byres I. of Tonley.

3. Elspet Byres (3rd dau. of James Byres II.
and Janet Middleton), bap. 31. Augt 1671.
John Christie, John Archibald, Wm Thomson, and Robert Gerard, godfathers.

In the pedigree of Croker of Rawleighstown, Co.
Limerick, vol. 8, p. 382 of the *Herald and Genealo-
gist*, a dau. of Edward Croker and Mary Buckner
married . . . . Byres.

III. ROBERT BYRES OF DUBLIN.

III. Robert Byres,[1] b. 1675, burgess of Aberdeen
(2nd son of James Byres of Aberdeen, and Janet
Middleton), settled first in Holland as a merchant.
Returning from there I find him witness to a service,
Dunbar, of Mill of Balcairn, Aberdeenshire, 10 May
1700 (Sheriff-Court Records). He married in Sept[r]
1704, Jean, dau. of Patrick Sandilands of Cotton,
near Aberdeen, by his 1st wife, Margaret, dau. of
William Ord of Cairnbee, in Fifeshire—see family of
Sandilands, p. 180. And Nov[r] 4, 1704, M[r] and Mrs
Byres went to Dublin—see register in Tonley family
Bible, p. 147. There Robert Byres " carried on a very
considerable trade, and both his credit and reputation
were very great, both at home and abroad."—Family
Memoir. He made his will, which is duly recorded
at Dublin, 6 May 1712—copy, see p. 186—and was
accidentally drowned in the Bay of Dublin shortly
after that date. His widow, Mrs. Jean Sandilands
or Byres, returned to Aberdeenshire ; and she, and
her late husband's trustees, bought from Alexander
Hay of Arnbath, the barony of Tonley in that county
(p. 82), 8th April 1718, of which place Patrick Garioch
was laird, 1695-6.—*Poll Book*. Mrs Jean Sandilands
was dead before 4 Aug[t] 1730. At that date her last
will and testament is recorded in the Commissary

[1] 1735, 2 Jany. Will given up by Patrick Byres of Tonley, only
executor, decerned as nearest of kin to him by decreet of the
Commissary of Edinburgh, 21 June 1734. Household furniture,
£100, &c. Cautioner, James Moir, son of M[r] Alexander Moir,
Professor of Philosophy, Edinburgh.

Books of Aberdeen. Issue, two sons and three daughters :—

1. James, born 27. Jany. 1709, died 19 May 1713, and was interred under the chancel of St. Mary's, Dublin.

2. Patrick, born 13. May 1713, his heir   Of him again (1ˢᵗ " Byres of Tonley ").

1. Margarete, born 17. Augᵗ 1705, died 24 Decʳ Family Bible. 1706, buried under the chancel of St. Mary's, See p. 146. Dublin.

2. Janet, born 25. Octʳ, and bap. 15 Novʳ 1706 ; died 5. Feby. 1709. Interred beside her sister.

3. Jean, born 24. Septʳ 1711, and bap. 12 Octʳ following.

IV. PATRICK BYRES, I. OF TONLEY.

"Marte suo tutus" (Safe by his own exertions).

IV. Patrick Byres (2d son of Robert Byres of Dublin, and Jean Sandilands), born at Dublin, 13 May 1713, I. of Tonley,—of this family,—became, through the extinction of the elder branch, representative of the Byres of Coates, in the county of Edinburgh, and as such registers his arms, 7 Feby.

Family Bible. 1755—see p. 142. Mr Byres m^d 14. June 1733, his relative, Janet, dau. of James Moir, M.P., of Stoneywood, on Donside, by his 2^d wife, Jean, dau. of Alexander Abernethy of Maye^n on Deveron side—see p. 82, county Banff—(see family of Moir of Stoneywood, p. 73); and Octr 8. same year, settled at

Register
of Tough. Tonley. Mrs Byres (who was buried at Tough, in which parish Tonley is, Septr 1787) was sister of Col. James Moir of Stoneywood—see that family, p. 73—one of the most zealous of the Stuarts' adherents. Patrick Byres, known as the "Jacobite Laird," was "out" in the "45," and engaged ardently in the cause of Charles Edward Stuart, and was a major in the regiment (known as "Stoneywood's Regt^t") raised by his brother-in-law, the above Col. James Moir.

"After fighting at the battle of Culloden, he was concealed in the Castle of Cluny, near Tonley, by his friend, Gordon of Cluny, until he got an opportunity of escaping to France. He entered into the regiment of Royal Scotch in France, commanded by Cameron of Lochiel, and was exempted from the

first pardon, and would have lost Tonley, but through
the interest of his friends it was made to appear that
the offending Jacobite was called Patrick and not
Peter Byres (as his name had been entered in the
list), therefore his estate was not liable to be confis-
cated, and he was eventually allowed to return to his
Highland home in Scotland." For some interesting
letters from Patrick Byres during his banishment in
France, &c.—see p. 169; and for the account of a duel
fought between John Leith of Leith Hall, and James
Abernethy of Mayen, in 1763, and in which Patrick
Byres was unfortunately mixed up—see p. 175.

From Memoir of James Young and Rachel Cruickshank, by my late worthy friend, Alexander Johnston, W.S.,—" It must have been a good many years
subsequent to the death, in 1763, of John Leith of
Leith Hall—see p. 175—that a quarrel arose between
a near kinsman of that gentleman, the late Alexander
Leith of Freefield and Glenkindie (father of the late
Mr Leith-Ross of Arnage—see p. 23), and Patrick
Byres of Tonley, at a meeting at Bridge of Alford,
of gentlemen connected with Donside. The alter-
cation is said to have originated as to a road re-
cently made in that vicinity, and which is understood
still to exist. High words having passed between
Freefield and Mr Byres, they left the inn at Bridge of
Alford, in which the company had met, and proceeded
to the green close by, where the two engaged in single
combat with the weapons which then formed part of
the every-day dress of persons of their rank. It is
not recorded that any bodily injury accrued to either
combatant ; they had, most probably, been speedily
separated by the interference of the rest of the company assembled on the occasion under notice. This

is said to have been the last rencontre in the way of duelling in that part of Scotland, in which the small sword was the weapon used. The exact date of the incident has not been ascertained, but it had likely taken place several years before the close of last century."

Patrick Byres (who was in June 1741 admitted a Burgess of Guild of Aberdeen) had issue by his wife, Janet Moir, four sons and three daughters, viz. :—

1. James, bap. 7. May 1734, his heir, II. of Tonley.

2. Robert of Kincraigie, bap. 12. Decr 1740, merchant, of Memel, in Prussia, and London. He bought the estate of Kincraigie[1] from the Leslies, 8. Decr 1786, which adjoins Tonley, and the old mansion of Kincraigie, with additions, is the present mansion-house of the property. " The auld hous," or part of it, is now the farm house of Mains of Tonley; and a stone, evidently belonging to it, bears the date, 1735. Robert Byres m^d his relative (contract dated 12. Novr 1770),

Margaret, dau. of James Burnett, merchant of Aberdeen, descended of the Dalladies branch of the house of Leys—see p. 181. He possessed considerable property at St. Pierre, Martinique, which he had gone to look after, and where he died, 17. Novr 1799. Issue, two sons and two daughters :—

---

[1] But the title was taken in favour of James Byres II. of Tonley, his brother, as specified in a deed dated Novr 1794.

1. James (from Reg. of parish of Tough).
   "1794, Sept' 24, Died, James Byres, son
   of Robert Byers, brother to the present
   M' James Byres of Tonley. The death
   of this young man was occasioned by an
   accidental discharge of a fowling-piece in
   the hands of his brother, Patrick Byres,
   while the two brothers were in the field
   shooting crows."

2. Patrick; of him again, as III. Byres of
   Tonley.

1. Isabella, m⁴ (as 2d wife) Lieut.-Col. James
   Stewart, of the 42ᵈ Highlanders, youngest
   son of Charles Stewart of Shambellie,
   in the Stewartry of Kirkcudbright. No
   issue.

2. Janet; died unmarried.

3. William, born 29. Oct' 1742. " He always was
   a delightful child. He served in the Navy ;
   was appointed one of the King's surveyors,
   and dyed in St. Vincent's in 1764-5. He
   always behaved well"—see Reg. in family
   Bible, p. 147. Tablet to his memory in
   church of Tough.

4. John, born 31. March 1745. A captain Royal
   Engineers, Hon. E. I. Co.'s Service. He
   made a fine model of Gibraltar, which is
   now in the Museum of the Royal Engineers
   at Chatham. Captain Byres married (contract dated 1ˢᵗ Oct' 1744) Isobel, dau. of
   James Donaldson, M.D., of Auchmull, by
   his wife, Katherine Gordon, of the family of
   Pitlurg—see Donaldson of Auchmull, p. 185

—and died 17. Septr 1788. Issue, two
daughters and co-heiresses :—

1. Katherine Byres, married, 1800, her cousin-
german, John Moir of St Catherine's,
Peterhead, artist, and had issue.—See
family of Moir, pp. 32, 33.

2. Janet Byres, married, 1802, her cousin-german, James Moir, M.D., elder brother
of John Moir of St. Catherine's, and had
issue.—See family of Moir, p. 36.

1. Jane, born 6. July 1735, married John Durno,
J.P., of Cattie, now Whitehouse, in the parish
of Tough, Aberdeenshire. Mr Durno, who
was b. 1741, was an advocate in Aberdeen.
At his decease, which occurred in the island of
Jamaica, in Decr 1816, he was the senior
member of the Society of Advocates of
Aberdeen, and also the oldest life manager
of the Royal Infirmary there. A brother of
his was Sir James Durno, Knight of Art-
rochie, H.M.B. Consul at Memel, in Prussia,
who died in 1807. Jane Byres or Durno
died without surviving issue.

2. Isabella, born 15. April 1737, married Robert
Sandilands, who is stated, on slender autho-
rity, to have been heir-presumptive to the
title of Torphichen. He had, more probably, been a relative of his wife's, a Sandilands of the Craibston, or Cotton families.
This lady, who also died without issue, was
killed by a fall from a pony carriage.

3. Martha, born 6. July 1739, married in 1766
the Revd Dr George Moir of Peterhead—
see family of Moir, p. 31—and had issue.

In the diary of the Rev⁴ John Bisset of Aberdeen, of which part is printed in Vol. I. of the Miscellany of the Spalding Club, occurs under date Feby. 3, 1746, the following paragraph:—" Yesterday, came in here from the south, Lonmay (William Moir), Tonlay (Patrick Byres, I. of Tonley), Robert Sandilands, Charles Moir, and one they call Captain Ferrier; and I am told four more gentlemen came at night whose names or designations I have not yet got."

JAMES BYRES, II. OF TONLEY.

Family Bible.   V. James Byres (eldest son of Patrick Byres I. of
Tonley, and Janet Moir of Stoneywood), II. of
Tonley, born 7. May 1734, and bap. by Mr Patrick
Laing; my Lord Forbes, godfather. Like his father,
this laird was a devoted Jacobite, and was for some
time an officer in Lord Ogilvie's regiment, under the
French king. Being mostly educated in France,
Mr Byres adopted the Roman Catholic faith. He
was much devoted to the fine arts, and was for
nearly forty years, before 1790, antiquarian resident
at Rome, and was author of " Hypogaei, or Sepul-
chral Caverns of Tarquinia," the capital of ancient
Etruria. The engravings in this work, which are very
fine, were executed by his nephew, Mr Christopher
Norton, who lived for many years with his uncle at
Rome.   It has always been understood in the family
that James Byres was a lay-cardinal at Rome, and a
fine oil painting of him, in his cardinal robes, is at
Tonley.   There is also, at least, another good picture of him there, as well as one at Castle Fraser,
the seat of the Mackenzie-Frasers, near Tonley.
But the finest portrait of this gentleman, by Raeburn, is now in the possession of Mr David Scott-
Moncrieff of Edinburgh. The following extracts
from " John Leech, and Other Papers," by John
Brown, M.D., the talented author of " Rab and his
Friends," &c., are interesting. On Sir Henry Raeburn, p. 420, " Byres, Barry's antagonist, gave him
an advice he ever after followed, and often spoke

about : ' Never paint any object from memory, if you
can get it before your eyes.' Again, speaking of Sir
Henry Raeburn's pictures, then 1882, at Charles-
field, Mid-Calder, near Edinburgh, the residence of
Sir Henry's grandson, L. W. Raeburn, at p. 432
Dr Brown says, " Besides many others, over the
fireplace is a life-size portrait of Mr Byres of Tonly,
whom we have mentioned as at Rome with Raeburn : this was painted long after, and is of the first
quality, done with the utmost breadth of felicity.
The ruffles of his shirt are still of dazzling whiteness,
as if bleached by the burn side."

According to the *Scots Magazine*, James Byres
left Rome in 1790, and died at Tonley, 3ᵈ Sepʳ 1817,
in his 84ᵗʰ year.

From Tough parish register : " 1796, Feb. 3,
James Byres of Tonley, and Robert Byres, Esq.,
residing there, were witnesses to the bap. of Patrick,
son of the Rev. Alexander Urquhart."

This laird united the two properties of Tonley
and Kincraigie, and entailed them on a series of
heirs, besides doing much to beautify and improve
these estates.

PATRICK BYRES, III. OF TONLEY.

VI. Patrick Byres, III. of Tonley (eldest surviving son of Robert Byres of Memel, and Margaret
Burnett), born circa 1778, was a major-general in
the Hon. E. I. Co.'s Service, succeeded to the
family property on the death of his uncle, James
Byres, in 1817; married, first, Jessie, dau. of Lieut.-
Col. Denny, and had an only son.

1. James, a lieut. in the 1st Royals; accidentally
drowned at Athlone, Ireland.

The General md 2ndly, in April 1834, his cousin-
german, Margaret, eldest dau. of Lieut.-Col. Joseph
Burnett of Gadgirth, Ayrshire, without issue,—see
family of Burnett,—and died 1st Feby. 1854, and was
interred at Tough, where there is a tombstone erected
to his memory. The succession then opened to the
next heir of entail, Patrick Moir, eldest son of
Katherine Byres, cousin-german of Gen. Byres, and
her husband, John Moir, of St. Catherine's. See
p. 33.

PATRICK MOIR-BYRES, IV. OF TONLEY.

VII. Patrick Moir Byres, IV. of Tonley (eldest
son of Katherine Byres, and her husband John Moir
of S⁺ Catherine's, see p. 33), b. 1802, succeeded
1854 his cousin General Byres, and assumed the
additional surname and arms of " Byres of Tonley " ;
was a Magistrate and Commissioner of Supply for
Aberdeenshire ; died at Tonley, unmarried, in 1863,
and was interred at Tough. He was succeeded by
his next brother.

JAMES GREGORY MOIR-BYRES, V. OF TONLEY.

James Gregory Moir-Byres, V. of Tonley. Born
17 Novr 1804 ; married in May 1858 Mary, dau. of
Henry Prideaux Hensleigh,[1] surgeon, of London, by
Mary Norrington, his wife, and relict of the Rev.
Thomas Gordon Torry Anderson (who was son of
Patrick Torry, Bishop of S⁺ Andrews, Dunkeld, and
Dunblane) of Fawsyde, Kincardineshire, sometime
incumbent of S⁺ Paul's, Dundee (to whom she had
one son, Alexander Penrose Torry Anderson, M.D.).

Mr Moir-Byres, who was a Magistrate and Commissioner of Supply for the county, bought the pro-

---

[1] The Hensleighs were long settled in the counties of Somer-
set and Devon. John Prideaux Hensleigh, grandfather of Mrs.
Moir-Byres, m^d a Prideaux of Lueson, an old Devonshire family
(Communicated by Mrs. James Moir-Byres.)

perty of Fairley from the Thomsons, in the parish of
Newhills, Aberdeenshire, and died at Aberdeen 6.
Novr 1881, and was interred at Tough, leaving an
only daughter and heiress, viz., Patricia Byres Moir-
Byres of Fairley, m^d 9 Decr 1879 Captain Harry
Vesey Brooke, formerly of the 92^d Gordon High-
landers, second son of the late Sir Arthur Brinsley
Brooke, Bart., of Colebrooke, county Fermanagh,
and the Hon. Henrietta Julia Anson. Issue, a son.

    1. James Anson Otho Brooke, b. 1884.

This laird was succeeded by his next brother.

GEORGE MOIR-BYRES, VI. OF TONLEY.

George Moir Byres, VI., and now of Tonley.
Born 1807 ; married 1854 Alleyne, dau. of Thomas
Houghton Fields of Colby, Lincolnshire, and has
issue three daughters, viz.—

    1. Alleyne Catherine Elizabeth, married 3^d Dec^r
        1881 Napier Macleod Wylie, of Edinburgh.

    2. Stuart.

    3. Jean.

Mr Moir-Byres is a Magistrate and Commissioner
of Supply for Aberdeenshire.

CADETS OF BYRES OF COATES.

I. Robert Byres, Burgess of Haddington, m^d Agnes Bromfield, who survived him, and died 2^d Novr 1593. Will given up by the said Agnes, his relict, and Mr George Byres, his son, who are his executors. Inventory, £364, 2s. [Edinbro' Wills.]

  1. Mr George, his heir, b. circa 1567.
  2. Andrew, who gets 50 merks under his father's will.
  1. Geills, gets same amount.
  2. Janet, gets 200 merks; m^d probably James Kirkwood, Burgess of Haddington; her will confirmed 27 Decr 1618, in which the following children are mentioned :—1. Robert; 2. George; and 1. Agnes; 2. Isobel; 3. Elspet Kirkwoods. [Ibid.]

II. The Revd George Byres, b. about 1567, M.A. St Andrews. Minister, 1st of Barra, 1589, afterwards of Legerwood, in Berwickshire, 1592. Died May 1640, aged about 73, and 51 ministry, and was succeeded by his son. [Scott's Fasti, Part ii. p. 527.]

III. The Revd Thomas Byres, b. circa 1606, M.A. (29 July 1626), of Legerwood. "Continued until 23 March 1653, when a process against him was to be given from hand to hand, and thought of before the meeting of Synod," &c.; and died in Feby. 1682. Issue, 5 sons. [Ibid.]

  1. George, the Rev^d, No. IV., his heir.
  2. "M^r" Thomas, marries, and has—

1. George, who gets 1000 merks and the books belonging to his uncle, Revd Geo. Byres No. IV., under his will dated in 1684.
2. Jean, who gets 300 merks under same document.
3. James
4. Robert } All mentioned in said will, 1684.
5. Joseph

IV. The Revd George Byres, M.A. (Glasgow University), of Lussuden, or St Boswell's. Licensed 10 March 1697 ; ordained 11 Aug^t ; died 16 Feby. 1730—"a judicious, plain, good man." M^d 26 April 1698 Lilias, dau. of Mark Gordon, in Cabertie ; gives up his will 22 April 1684, and it is recorded 12 June 1688. Appoints Lilias Gordon, "his dearly loving wife," his sole executrix. Cautioner, George Gordon, son to Thomas Gordon, Sheriff-Clerk of Aberdeen.[1]

V. The Revd George Byres, M.A., of St Boswell's, having succ^d his father therein. Lic. 1 Decr 1724 ; ord. 24 Septr 1730. M^d 16 Novr 1732 Jean, dau. of the Revd Gabriel Wilson of Maxton ; "suspended 1738, having adopted independant principals."

Scott's
Fasti.

I. Michael Byres, burgess of Hamilton, in 1618 gets obligation from Archibald Hamilton, of Marritoun, also mentioned in 1619, 1622, &c.,—see p. 163— brother of Matthew and Andrew Byres, of Hamilton,

---

[1] His son, Mr George, gets otherwise half of his estate, the other half to be divided amongst the rest of his children.

see p.   (and also probably of John Byres I. of
Coates).

    1. Michael—mentioned in deed 1618, see p. 163.

    2. James, died Decr 1634. Will given up 6. June
        1635, by Janet Douglas, his relict, who is by
        it appointed "tutor to bairn yet unborn," [1]
        "along with Mr John Scougal of Humbie,
        East Lothian, John Peirson, merchant-bur-
        gess of Edinburgh, and Donald Bain Bowar
        (bowmaker), burgess of Edinburgh. By his
        will he leaves £100 to be distributed
        among poor of Edinbro," and 100 merks to
        the Trinity Hospital of Edinburgh.

    3. Matthew, merchant-burgess of Edinburgh, died
        1645, gets 500 merks from the above brother
        James, by his will; [2] M^d Issobel Nisbet.
        Will confirmed 12. May 1646, and given up
        by Janet Byres, relict of Robert Dobie,
        tailor-burgess of Edinburgh. Issue, four sons
        and four daughters, viz.:—

        1. John, who gets 100 merks under the will of
            Margaret Barclay, wife of John Byres, I.
            of Coates, designed "eldest son" in his
            uncle's will, and as such to succeed to
            the "500 merks" after his father.

        2. George, bap. 26. March 1623. Witnesses,
            George Fowlis, and Mr Gilbert Prym-
            rose.

---

[1] This child, Beatrix Byres, bap. 3. Feby. 1635,—Witnesses,
John Pearsone, mert., Wm Gray, Johne Slowen, John Liddaill,
merchts., and Donald Bayne Bower,—is served heir-general of her
father in 1635, July 16.—*Retours,*

[2] Amongst the debtors in this document, are John Smyth,
Provost of Edinburgh, and Janet his spouse—Thomas Somerville,
£25, "for a ¼ths board of Isobell Moffat, daughter to Col.
Moffat."

3. William, bap. 11. Feby. 1628. Witnesses, W^r Makmath, elder and y^r, and Wm Nisbet.

4. Matthew, bap. 17. March 1637. Witnesses, John Pearsone, John Liddaill, James Nicoll, merch^t, Robert Dobie, tailor.

1. Agnes, bap. 20. June 1619. Wm Nisbet, a witness.

2. Margaret, bap. 27. Decr 1629. Witnesses, Mr Robt Burnet, Mr John Pearsone.

3. Isobell, bap. 3. June 1632. Witnesses, John Pearsone, Ja^s Makmath, John Liddail, and Wm Nisbet, merchants.

4. Janet (eldest dau.), gets 100 merks in will dated 1616 of Margaret Barclay, wife of John Byres, I. of Coates, m^d 12. April 1631 Robert Dobie, burgess-tailor of Edinburgh, (was dead defore 1646). Issue—

1. Isobel Dobie, bap. 3. June 1632. Witnesses, Wm Makmath, Chas Hammiltoun, Ja^s Dobie, and Matthew Byres, merchants.

2. Barbara Dobie, bap. 22. Septr 1633. Ja^s Dobie, and Matthew Byres.

3. Robert Dobie, bap. 20. Dec. 1635. Witnesses, Robt Dobie, Chas Hamilton, John Pearsone, Matthew Byres, John Liddell.

4. Issobell, bap. 1. May 1638. Henrie Nisbet, John Littlejohn, witnesses.

5. Janet, bap. 11. June 1640.

6. Rebecca.

4. James, (showing that sometimes two brothers were called by the same christian name), left by *his brother James*, 1634, " the sum of which is due to me by   Leith."

PEARSONS.

Margaret Byres (daughter of Michael Byres, burgess of Hamilton) married John Pearsone, merchant-
burgess of Edinburgh (of the family of " Pearsone of
Balmades," in Forfarshire). She died 23. March
1648. Among the debtors is mentioned John Byres,
son lawful to the late Matthew Byres, merchant-burgess of Edinbro, see former page. Of Debts, £500
to Sir Wm Dick of Braid, "for customs on wines"—
16 tuns of French wine being in their possession,—
"and for freight of same to skippers from Leith harbour, £400." Issue, three sons and four daughters:—

1. Edward, bap. 8. April 1623. Witnesses, Adam Edinburgh Wills and Registers.
   and James Pearson, &c.
2. Thomas, bap. 9. June 1625. Mr Thos Sidserff,
   Thos Chartres, Thos Cleghorn, Thos Pearson.
3. James, bap. 2. Novr 1626 (merchant-burgess of
   Edinburgh, executor to his mother). Witnesses, John Byres, Edward Edgar, Maister
   James Pearsone, James Pearsone, of Balmades, and Ja^s Pearsone, in Craigie.

1. Agnes, bap. 16. Novr 1620. Witnesses, John
   Byres, Mr Alex^r Pearson, and Thos Chartres.
2. Rachel, bap.   1622. Witnesses, M^r
   Thos Sidserff, and Thos Charteris.
3. Bessie, bap. 18. April 1624. Witnesses, M^r
   Alex^r and Adam Pearsone.
4. Issobell, bap. 13. February 1628. Arch^d Tod,
   Ed^w Edgar, and James Pearsone of Balmades.

LIDDELS, WILSONS, &c.

Agnes Byres (I take to be another dau. of Michael Byres, burgess of Hamilton) m^d 26. Octr 1625 James Liddel, burgess-tailor of Edinburgh. Issue—

1. Michael, bap. 20. Augt 1626. Witnesses, Michael Gibson, Jo^n Forrest, Ja^s Russell.
2. Andrew, bap. 19. Decr 1627. Witnesses, And^w Whyte, Michael Gibsone, Ro^t Crightoun.
3. James, bap. 2. June 1635. Witnesses, Mr Ja^s Chein, Ja^s Keyth , Geo. Marshall, Alex^r Hay, tailors.
1. Margaret, bap. 13. June 1630.
2. Anna, bap. 2. Jany. 1633.

Janet Byres (probably another dau. of Michael Byres of Hamilton) m^d 4. June 1646 Gilbert Wilson, merchant-burgess of Edinburgh.

1. Johnne, bap. 7. March 1647. Witnesses, John Pearsone, John Liddaill, merts., Michael Gibson, tailor.
2. Alexander, bap. 10. Octr 1650. Witnesses, John Pearsone, John Littlejohn, merchts., John Reid, and David Durie.
1. Margaret, bap. 17. Octr 1652. Witnesses, John Pearsone, baillie, John Anderson, banker, Ja^s Chalmers, mercht., John Grenlays.

Archibald Laurie, merchant, and Margaret Byres. m^d 1. June 1620.

Richard Byres, miller or maltman, burgess of

Edinburgh (perhaps another brother of John Byres, I. of Coates, &c.,) is witness in 1621 to a charter in favour of the said John Byres, of the Kirkland of the Glebe of St. Cuthbert's,—see p. 161. M^d 1st, Margaret Fleeming (Fleming).

1. Johne, bap. 4. May 1623. Witnesses, Johne Byres, Johne Mowat, and James Chalmers. Edinburgh City Parish Registers.
2. James, bap. 13. May 1627. Witnesses, Ja^s Chalmers, Ja^s Smyth, and Jo^n Smyth.
1. Helene, bap. 24. March 1625. Witnesses, Ja^s Chalmers, merch^t, and Ja^s Whyte, maltman, Richard Byres, and Agnes Vaitch (Veitch), m^d 6. Decr 1627.
2. Catherine, bap. 27. June 1630. Witnesses, John Walker, Dav. Bartleman.

Andrew Byres (another brother of Michael Byres of Hamilton, &c.,) m^d Janet Smyth, (who died July 1579), her will[1] confirmed 25. Feby. 1580.

1. Andrew, ⎱ appointed her executors, and failing Ibid., and Wills.
2. James, ⎰ them their brother Michael.
3. Michael.
4. John, to whom she,—Janet Smyth, his mother— leaves " her part of gear," and describes him as " her youngest son."
1. Catherine, m^d .... Hamilton, gets £10 under her mother's will.

I. James Byres, indweller in Hamilton, dead before 1620, m^d and had a son.

1. Robert, described at that date as " younger, merchant."—See p. 163.

[1] Robert and Isobel Byres, mentioned in will, get two bolls of meal.

William Byres, servant to John Byres, I. of Coats, is the writer of a deed 1622. See p. 163.

A servant apprentice, or secretary, of this kind was, at the period, often a near relative of his master.

James Byres, servant to John Byres, I. of Coates, 1630. p. 164.

Thomas Byres in Scarlaw, West Lothian, 1621, p. 163.

Agnes Byres, m⁴ James Riddell, burgess-tailor of the Canongate. He died in Decʳ 1661, she 1662. For copy of their will, which is curious, see p. 152.

James Byres, wobster in Burnside, par. of Ebdie, Fife, died Augᵗ 1601. Agnes Smith, his wife, appointed only executrix. Thomas Byres, his brother, gets "his work loom, and best cloak : the rest of his clothing and graifth," to Archibald and William Byres. Thomas Smith, burgess of Edinburgh, cautioner. Free estate, £2,055.

Retours, 2336, xiv. 168.
1637, Novʳ 30, John Byris, served heir of John Byris in Coulter Manes (in Lanarkshire), his grandfather.

I. William Byres, cordiner. Will recorded 12. June 1688, by,

Edinbro' Wills.
(1.) Adam Byres, cordiner in the Water of Leith, his son. He died 17. Octʳ 1712. Will recorded 2. Decʳ following, given up by Thomas Byres, weaver of Bellsmill (probably his brother), executor appointed by decreit of the commissary of Edinburgh, at

the instance of the said Thomas Byres, against William Byres, son of the said Adam Byres. Cautioner both in 1688 and 1712, Matthew Byres, weaver at Bellsmill, Water of Leith.

Probably of the last branch—

James Byres, weaver in St. Cuthbert's, m^d Margaret Fortune.
    1. William, 19. Jany. 1651. Witnesses, Wm Byres, weaver, John Chrystie, clothier.

William Byres, in St. Cuthbert's, m^d 1. Decr 1641. Margaret Bennet.
    1. Issobell, 16. Feby. 1651. Witnesses, Patrick Hepburne, brewer, and Johne Byris, weaver.

John Byris, in West Kirk, m^d Janet Cööse.
    1. Johne, 20. April 1651.

James Byres, cordiner or shoemaker, m^d Janet Meaklejohne.
    1. Johne, 30. Octr 1653. Witnesses, Patrick Meaklejohne, baxter, and John Doogood, &c. &c.
    2. Johne, 1655.
    3. Issobell, 23. May 1658.

ARMS OF THE SURNAME OF BYRES, FROM THE
LYON REGISTERS, &c.

1625-49.   In "Gentleman's Arms," a collection dating from the reign of
Charles I.—
    Byres, azure on a chevron, between three bees volant, argent,
a crescent, gules.

1661.   From MS. of Arms by Robert Porteous, Snowdon Herald—
Byres, of Strathaven (in Lanarkshire), azure, a chevron argent,
between three bees volant, arrieree, or.
    He gives the same for Sir John Byres of Coates, with the motto,
"Rule be One." The crest as given in Fairbairn is a bee, as in
the arms.
    The Byres arms impaled with the arms of Smith of Groithill,
viz., azure, a burning cup, or, are so depicted on the monument
to John Byres of Coates, in the Greyfriars' Churchyard, Edinburgh,
who died in 1639. Mr R. R. Stodart, the talented author of
"Scottish Arms," &c., in that valuable work says :—"In 1755,
arms were registered by Patrick Byres of Tonley, in Aberdeenshire, stated to be representative of 'the family of Coatts,'
—azure, a chevron, argent, between three martlets volant, or.
Why the bees were changed to martlets it is difficult to see, as
they are distinctly drawn and described in several verbal blazons."

1755   "Patrick Byres, Esquire of Tonley, in vicecomitatu de Aberdeen, descended from Sir John Byres of Coatts, in vicecomitatu
Laudoniæ, and now representing the said family of Coatts, bears,
azure, a chevron, argent, between three martlets volant, or. Crest,
a cock reguardant proper. Motto, 'Marte suo Tutus.'—Matriculated, 7th Feby. 1755."

I.—From EPITAPHS and MONUMENTAL INSCRIPTIONS, Greyfriars' Churchyard, Edinburgh (JAMES BROWN).

JOHN BYRES OF COITTES' TOMB.

1629. Vivo vere probo, civi optimo, Joanni Byres, de Coittes, urbis hujus anno ex ordine sex quaestori : duos ballivo et ex ballivo, sex aedile, et duos pro praefecto : familiare hoc monumentum posuerunt uxor A. S. et liberi : obiit multum desideratus, viii. Kal, Decemb. anno salutis MDCXXIX., aetatis suae LX.

Translation.

To a man truly good, an excellent citizen, John Byres of Coittes, six years together thesaurer of the city, two years city bailie and suburban bailie, six years Dean of Guild, and two years Old Provost—his wife, A. S., and his children, have erected this homely monument. He died, much lamented, 24th November, the year of Christ 1629, and of his age the 60 year.

Copy of Inscription on Tombstone, St. Nicholas Churchyard, Aberdeen.

Here lyes (in hopes of) a Blessed Resurrection, Janet Midleton, spouse to James Byres, Merchant in (Aberdeen, who) departed this life 26 November 1695, and of her age 58 (years).

II.—"WARRAND to the MAGISTRATES of ST ANDROIS for secureing thir prisoneris following" (amongst whom is Sir John Byres).

(From General Index to Acts of Parliament of Scotland.)

1645. The estates of Parliament ordanes the Magistratis of St. Androis To provyde roumes vpon th awne charges and expe^{ss} for thir prisoners, vis., the Lord Seytoun, the Lord drūmond, the laird of Rosyth, . . . Spottiswode, y^r of dairsie, Mr. Laurence

rollok, Sr Johne byire, Mr. Patrik hay, and fyve udre wha ar the
servands, and came in th^r companie.

And to keip the saids persones in the samen rowmes w^t sufficient
guardis; and ordanes the magistrats to be ans^table for them q^{ll}
Friday next inclusive upon th^r highest perell.

III.—POSTNUPTIAL CONTRACT between JOHN BYRES of COATES and LILIAS GRANT of Grant (or that Ilk), 1666.

From Fraser's History of the "Chiefs of Grant," vol. iii., pp. 463 and 464.

1666. *Contract between* JOHN BYRES *of Coates, and* LILIAS GRANT, *lawful daughter to the deceased* [JAMES] GRANT *of that Ilk, as follows :—*

JOHN BYRES, for fulfilling his part of the agreements made and concurred in before the marriage solemnised between him and Lilias Grant, and for other causes to be shortly stated, becomes bound with all possible diligence to infeft and sease his said spouse in liferent in all and whole the annual rent of ten chalders good and sufficient bear, with a hundred and twenty pounds Scots for the rent of a dwelling-house to her to dwell in, to be uplifted in equal portions at Whitsunday and Martinmas, free of all teind duties, minister's stipends, or other burdens whatsoever, forth of all and whole the lands of Coates, comprehending the lands, acres, tenements, superiorities, and others mentioned in John Byres's infeftment of the same, with houses and pertinents thereof, in the regality and barony of Broughtoune, and sheriffdom of Edinburgh, or forth of any portion of these lands, and readiest maills and duties of the same, by double charters and infeftments, the one to be held of John Byres and his heirs, and the other of the immediate superiors of the lands, in free blench farm, for the yearly payment of one penny if asked, he also binding himself to complete, seal, subscribe, and deliver to Lilias charters and other necessary writs to that effect, containing ample warrandice in the manner afterwards laid down ; also John Byres becomes bound to warrant and defend the above infeftments in all the terms of them as there specified, in liferent, from all perils, dangers, and inconveniences whatsoever, whereby Lilias might be hindered or prejudged in the peaceable possession of the same. John Byres further comes under obligation to provide to the heirs-male procreated between them as much of the lands and estate of Coates as will extend in yearly rent to ten chalders of bear; and if there should only be female heirs, to divide the ten chalders of bear among them, by the advice of one or two friends chosen by either of the parties, by whose advice the heirs-female referred to are obliged to marry—entry to the rents and duties of the ten chalders to be at the first term of Whitsunday or Martinmas after his decease. In the mean time, John Byres binds himself to sustain, entertain, educate, and upbring the foresaid children in a manner becoming their rank and estate; providing that if George Byres, his eldest son, shall depart this life, so that the children had between John and Lilias shall succeed to the whole estate, the obligation to provide ten chalders of bear shall be null; and in case of such event, John Byres binds himself to add to the liferent provision of Lilias, his spouse, the manor-place of Coates, with the houses, buildings, pertinents, and others belonging thereto, in lieu of the one hundred and twenty pounds, together with a yearly duty of three chalders of victual further to be uplifted of the lands and at the terms before stated, to be over and above the ten chalders of bear already provided to her in liferent, which additions are to be made over to her in liferent in double infeftment, to be held, and with warrandice, in manner as aforesaid. He also binds himself that where he shall acquire any lands, heritages, or others during the period of his marriage, he will acquire the half thereof to Lilias in liferent, and the whole of the same to the heirs procreated of them in fee—which liferent provision Lilias accepts in full satisfaction of all conjunct fee, liferent, terce, or third of all lands, heritages, goods, and others which shall pertain to John at his decease, without prejudice to Lilias of her third of the moveables of John's dwelling-house, and insight and plenishings thereof, which is reserved to her. Lilias, on her part, constitutes and ordains John Byres, her husband, and his heirs, her undoubted and irrevocable cessioners and assignees in and to all debts, sums of money, bond of provision, goods, gear, and others which she shall in any way fall heir to, or which shall pertain to her, dispensing with a more particular enumeration of the same, and declaring the present assignation thereto in all respects

T

effectual and sufficient, giving him power to receive and intromit with the debts, sums of money, and others, and to dispone and use the same at his pleasure, and to do all other things therewith which she could have done before the date of this contract, with precept of sasine in favour of Lilias, and clause of registration. The contract is dated at Coupar of Fyfe, 26th May 1666, and is subscribed by John Byres and Lilias Grant. The witnesses are George, Marquise of Huntly, W. Scott of Ardross, John Saintsery, doctor of medicine, Major William Arnot, Andrew Patersone of Kilmonie, and Captain Francis Stewart. The deed is also signed by Marie, Marchioness of Huntly, sister of Lilias Grant, although she is not otherwise mentioned in it.

IV.—From OLD FAMILY BIBLE at TONLEY.

1775. Copy from a Note in my Father's (viz., Robert Byres, of Dublin) Bible.

1704. In September I was married to Mrs Jean Sandilands, daughter to Patrick Sandilands, Esq., of Cotton, and November 4th we arrived at Dublin.

1705. August 17. My wife was brought to bed of a daughter, who was the same day christened by the name of Margarete.

1706. 25th of October. My wife was brought to bed of a daughter, who was christened the 15th of November by the name of Janett. 24th December. Our eldest daughter, Margarete, dyed of chincough and teething, and was buried under the Chancell at St. Mary's (Dublin).

1709. 27th, at night (at 11). My wife was brought to bed of a son, who was christened by the name of James. February 5th Dyed our daughter Janett, and was buried by her sister in the Chancell at St. Mary's. She died of a fever.

1711. Monday, the 24th September. My wife was brought to bed of a daughter, who was christened on the 12th of October by the name of Jean.

1713. Wednesday, the 13th of May. My wife was brought to bed of a son, 'twixt 9 and 10 at night, who was christened

Patrick on the 1st June. On the 19th of the same
month, dyed our eldest son, James, and was buried by
his two sisters under St. Mary's Chancell.

Follows an Account of our own Family (*Patrick Byres*) of *Tonley*.

1733. I was married to Mrs. Janet Moir, daughter to James Moir,
Esq. of Stoneywood, and October the 8th we came to
Tonley, N.B. We were married the 14th June.

1734. May 7th. My wife was brought to bed of a son, who was
christened by the name of James by Mr. Patrick Laing,
my Lord Forbes godfather.

1735. July 6th. My wife was brought to bed of a daughter; same
day was christened by the name of Jane.

1737. April 15th. My wife was brought to bed of a daughter, who
same day was christened by the name of Isabella.

1739. July 6th. My wife was brought to bed of a daughter, who
was christened by the name of Martha.

1740. Friday, December 12. My wife was brought to bed of a son.
He was next day christened by the name of Robert.

1742. October 29. My wife was brought to bed of a son. He
was next day christened by the name of William. He
always was a delightful child. He served in the Navy,
was appointed one of the King's surveyors, and dyed in
St. Vincent's in 1764-65. He always behaved well.

1745. March 31. My wife was brought to bed of a son, who was
christened by the name of John.

19th August 1595.   Guild Register,
                                                     Vol. 2.

The same day in presens of Alexander Vddert dene of gild and   19 August
his counsall Jhone Byres merchant prenteis to John Robertsoun 1595.
merchant comperand sufficientlie airmit with ane furneist hagbut
is maid burges of this burgh he richt of his prenteiship and hes
gewin his aith. . . . and hes payit to the dene of gild   - v lib.

In presens of John Robertsoun deyne of gild and the gild coun- 24 March
                                                                1601.

sale Johnne Byris merchand burges of before is maid gild brother of this burgh, . . . and hes payit - - - - - x lib

Guild Register Vol. 2.
16 September 1607.

In presens of the above Matthew Byris merchant prenteis to Johne Byris merchant burges and gildbrother. . . . is maid burges and gild brother. . . . be richt of his said prenteiship. . . . and hes payit - - - - - - - - xv lib

Vol. 3.
4 August 1619.

In presens of David Aikinheid deyne of gild and the gild counsell Richard Byris merchand. . . . is maid burges. . . . be richt of Margaret Fleyming his spous lawchfull dochter to Robert Fleyming maltman burges of the samyne. . . . and hes payit
xiij⁵ iiij ᵈ

4 October 1620.

John Byris, Dean of Guild.

3 August 1653.

James Byris cordiner compeirand is made burges. . . . as prenteis first to wmquhile Andro Greir and nixt to Thomas Herpar cordiners burgesses of the samen. . . . and payit   v lib Thomas Herpar becomes suretie.

4 January 1660.

Alexander Byres merchant. . . . made burges and gildbrother. . . . as sone lawfull to wmquhill Johne Byrs of Coatts merchant burges and gildbrother therof. . . . and hes payed - xxxiij⁵ iiij ᵈ

3 October 1662.

John Byres of Coats and Mr. Robert Byres advocate compeirand are made burgesses and gild brether. . . . conforme to ane act of the provest bailyies and councill of the date the tuelt day of September last. . . . and paid. . . . each of them which is repayed be the said act -   -   -   - j ᶜ lxvj ˡⁱᵇ xiij⁵ iij ᵈ

Commissariot of Edinburgh.

Testaments.

Vol. 49.
17 April 1616.

Margaret Barclay spouse to John Byris merchant burgess of Edinburgh.

The Testament Testamentar and Inventar of the guidis geir sowmes of money and debtis pertening to vmquhile Margaret Barclay sumtyme spous to Johne Byris merchand burges of Edinburgh the tyme of hir deceis quha deceist upone the xxij day of January the yeir of God 1616 yeiris ffaithfullie maid and gevin up be the said Johne Byris hir spous as father and laufull administrator to Agnes Byris minor hir youngest dochter quhome scho nominatis hir

onlie executrix in hir lattrewill underwryttine in presens of
Maister Johne Haliday advocat James Dalyell and Johne
Barclay merchandis burgessis of Edinburgh witnessis.

In the ffirst the said vmquhile Margaret Barclay and hir said
spouse had the guidis geir sowmes of money and debtis of the
availl and prices efter following pertening to thame the tyme of
hir deceis foirsaid Videlicet Item in ventar with James Wrycht
to   foure lastis hering at ane hundreth pundis the
last suma iiijᶜ lib. Item in wenture with Johne Piersone the
sowme of thrie hundreth pundis Item in venture with Johne
Linkvp the sowme of iijᶜ lib. Item the aucht pairt of Johne
Linkvp schip with hir ornamentis effeirand thairto estimat to the
sowme of Thrie hundreth pundis Item of reddie money the sowme
of vᶜ merkis ffollowis the silwer werk by the airschip Videlicet
Item ane silwer saltfull weyand sex vnce weycht price of the vnce
weycht iijˡⁱᵇ suma xviijˡⁱᵇ Item foure silwer coupis weyand all
xxxvj vnces price of the vnce weycht thrie pundis suma ane hundreth aucht pundis Item sex silwer spones weyand all nyne vnce
weycht price of the vnce weycht thrie pundis suma xxvijˡⁱᵇ Item
in vtenceilis and domiceilis by the airschip with the abulzementis
of hir body estimat to the sowme of ijᶜ lib.

Suma of the Inventar   -   -   -   jᵐ ixᶜ lxxxvj ˡⁱᵇ vjˢ viijᵈ

ffollowis the debtis awin to the dead.

Item thair wes awin to the said vmquhile Margaret Barclay and
hir said spous be Maister Johne Duncane minister at Liff jᶜ lib.
Item be Stephane Phillope jˡⁱᵇ Item be Maister Johne Russell
advocat fyftie pundis Item be Johne Arnot commissar clark of
Sanctandrois xxxiijˡⁱᵇ vjˢ viijᵈ Item be Maister Henry Russell
and William   Twentie sex pundis xiijˢ iiijᵈ Item
be Maister David Wod lxvjˡⁱᵇ xiijˢ iiijᵈ Item be Maister Henry
Russell and Johne Gray lxvjˡⁱᵇ xiijˢ iiijᵈ Item be Johne Scheveis
guidman of   lxvjˡⁱᵇ xiijˢ iiijᵈ Item be Maister
Alexander Gledstanes lxvjˡⁱᵇ xiijˢ iiijᵈ Item be James Tulloch
and Johne Browne in   xvˡⁱᵇ vˢ iiijᵈ Item be William M'Cairtnay sex barrellis hering at aucht pundis the barrell
suma xlviijˡⁱᵇ Item be George Smyth elder merchand jᶜ lib. Item
be Alexander Erle of Drumfermeling Lord Chansler vjᶜ lxvjˡⁱᵇ
xiijˢ iiijᵈ Item be George Thomsone ane hundreth thriescoir
sex pundis xiijˢ iiijᵈ Item be Walter Smyth in Elgeine iijᶜ xx ˡⁱᵇ

Item be Maister Robert Bruce ane hundreth pundis Item be
Johne Corstoune in Crawmond for relieff of Maister Mark Mawer
and the rest bund with him twa hundreth pundis Item be
Thomas Lindsay and Johne Conynghame or ather of thame tua
hundreth xl^{lib} Item be Daniell Ros in Tayne ane hundreth vj^{lib}
xiij^s iiij^d Item be   guidman of Quhytbank as
assignay lauchfullie constitute be Gilbert Bannatyne and Jeane
Jonstoune ane hundreth xvij^{lib} Item be Thomas Diksone ventiner
for wynes v^c lxxxx^{lib} Item be Gilbert Dik ventiner for wynes
v^c xl^{lib} Item be Henry Seytoune for wyne iiij^c iiij^{lib} Item be
Anthonie Goisleine litster for waid ij^c lxxxviij^{lib} Item be Johne
Andersone elder litster burges of Drumfermling for waid ij^c
lxxxviij^{lib} Item be James Glen litster for waid iij^c lxxxxij^{lib} Item
be the Laird of Innermarkie the defunct and hir said spous fourt
pairt of ane blok of wictuall estimat to the sowme of ane thow-
sand ij^c lxxv^{lib} Item be the Laird of Govye the defunct and hir
said spous   pairt of ane blok of wittuall coft fra him
estimat to the sowme of ane thowsand pundis Item be Andro
Scot merchand and his cautioneris the sowme of thretteine hun-
dreth xxxiij^{lib} vj^s viij^d Item be   and remanent
tennentis and occupyeris of his landis of Coitis resten of the price
of thair firmes and dewties thairof ane thowsand ij^c xxxiij^{lib}
vj^s viij^d Item be the Laird of Airth fyve hundreth pundis resten
of the price of Coilis Item be the proveist baillies counsell and
cowmowntie of the burgh of Edinburgh the sowme of iiij^m lib.

Suma of the debtis awin to the dead xiiij^m v^c l^{lib} xij^s
Suma of the Inventar with the debtis xvj^m v^c xxxvj^{lib} 18^s 8^d

ffollowis the debtis awin be the dead.

Item thair wes awin be the said vmquhile Margaret Barclay and
hir said spous To Johne, Alexander, Robert and James Kincaidis
bairnes of vmquhile Clement Kincaid of the Coitis or ony of
thame haveand best rycht conforme to ane contract resten of the
price of the landis of Coitis the sowme of iiij^m viij^c pundis Item
to Maister Thomas Sydeserff resten of tocherguid with
Byris thair dochter the sowme of foure thowsand pundis Item be
         Barclay Laird of Towie resten of the price of
wictuall v^c lib Item to Johne Barclay merchand in Edinburgh of
borrowit money sex hundreth thriescar sex pundis xiij^s iiij^d Item
to George Suttie merchand for merchandice thrie hundreth pundis
quhilk is payit sen the defunctis deceis Item to Thomas Dun-

cane smyth for irne wark ane hundreth aucht pundis quhilk is
payit sen the defunctis deceis.

Suma of the debtis awin be the dead - x^{m} iij^{c} lxxiiij^{lib} 13^{s} 4^{d}
Restis of ffrie geir the debtis deducit - vj^{m} j^{c} lxij^{lib} v^{s} 4^{d}
To be devydit in thrie pairtis Deadis
pairt is - - - - - ij^{m} liiij^{lib} j^{s} ix^{d}
Quhairof the quot is componit for - lxviij^{lib}

ffollowis the deadis Legacie and Lattrewill.

At Edinburgh the twentie ane day of January 1616 yeiris. The
quhilk day Margaret Barclay spous to Johne Byris merchand
burges of the said burghe being viseit with seiknes and infirmitie
of hir bodie yit perfyte of memorie and senssis knawing nathing
mair certane nor death nor uncertane nor the hour and tyme
thairof and hoiping to be saved be the blude of Jesus Cryst commitis hir saule to his blissed protexioune makis hir testament and
lattrewill as followis To wit as concerning the vpgeving of the
Inventar of the guidis geir and debtis and utheris pertening to hir
and to the said Johne Byris hir spous scho referris the vpgeving
thairof to the said Johne Item scho nominatis makis and con-
stitutis Agnes Byris hir youngest dochter hir onlie executrix and
universall intromissatrix with hir guidis and geir Item scho leives
in legacie to hir twa oyes Margaret and Bessy Heriotis laufull
bairnes to Alexander Heriot procreat betwix him and Margaret
Byris his dochter ilk ane of thame the sowme of fyve hundreth
merkis Item scho leives to the first bairne gif ony sall happin to
be gottine betwix Maister Thomas Sydeserff minister and Rachaell
Byris hir secund dochter the sowme of fyve hundreth merkis Item
scho leives to Jonet and Johne Byris laufull bairnes to Mathow
Byris burges of the said burghe of Edinburgh ilkane of thame ane
hundreth merkis Item scho leives to the hospitall of Edinburgh
ane hundreth pundis and to the pure thairof xx^{lib} and willis thir
legacies abonewryttine to be payit be the said John hir husband
quhen he may convenientlie do the same and his dettis being ffirst
payit In witnes of the quhilk thing subscryvit be the notar underwryttine at my command becaus I can not wryt my selff day yeir
place and before the witnessis abone specefeit sic subscribitur Ita
est Robertus Kirkwod notarius publicus in premissis requisitus de
mandato dicte Margarete Barclay teste manu propria.

We Maisteris Johne Airthour etc. and geives and commitis the
intromissioune with the samyne to the said Agnes Byris onlie

executrix testamentar nominat be the said vmquhile Margaret
Barclay hir mother Reservand compt etc. and Johne Byris hir
father in respect of hir minoritie being sworne maid faith etc.
Alexander Heriot merchand burges of Edinburgh his sone in law
cautiounear ane act maid thairvpon beiris.

TESTAMENT DATIVE and INVENTORY of JAMES RIDDELL, Tailor Burgess of the Canongate, Edinburgh.

Commissariot
of Edinburgh.

Testaments.

Vol. 70.
12 July 1662.

JamesRiddell,
tailor burgess
of the Canon-
gate, Edin-
burgh.

The Testament Dative and Inventar of the goodes geir sowmes
of moneyes and debts perteaning to vmquhill James
Riddell taylor burges of the Cannongate and vmquhill
Agnes Byres his spous and the deceist Androw Riddell
thair sone the tyme of thair respective deccissis Quha
deceist videlicet the said vmquhill James Riddell in the
month of Jy. j^m vj^c of yeirs the said vmquhill Agnes Byres
in the moneth of Jy. last by past 1662 yeirs instant and the
said deceist Andrew Riddell in the moneth of December
1661 yeirs ffaithfullie maid and given vp be Walter Riddell
wryter in Edinburgh only Executor Dative surrogat to the
said vmquhill defunct in place of the procuratour fiscall be
decreit of the commissars of Edinburgh As the samyne of
the daitt at Edinburgh the   day of July 1662 yeirs at
mair lenth proports.

In the first the saids vmquhill James Riddell Agnes Byres and
Andro Riddell thair sone had the goodes and geir following of the
availls and pryces afftermentioned perteaning to thame the tyme of
their respective deceissis abovementionat videlicet Imprimis the
whole insight and plennishing of thair duelling house with the air-
schipe and all vther small plennisching thairin estimat all in
cumulo to the sowme of ij^c xl^{lib} scottes money.
Suma of the Inventar   -   -   -   -   - ij^c xl^{lib} scotts

ffollowes the debts awine to the deid.

Item thair wes restand awand to the said vmquhill James
Riddell Agnes Byres and Andrew Riddell the tyme of thair
respective deceissis abovementionat at ieist to ane or vther of
thame the particular debts and sowmes of money following   To
witt be James Keith laufull sone to vmquhill Alexander Keith

wryter be band ij^c lx^{lib} Be the said Walter Riddell executour
foirsaid v^c marks Be the Laird of Smeattoune be compt xix^{lib}
xix^s Be Cristiane Dowglas v^{lib} Be John Clark vij^{lib} xvij^s Be
Anna Watsoune xviij^{lib} xxij^s Be Margaret Sydserff xix^{lib} xviij^s Be
Alexander Rig xviij^{lib} xvj^s Be Mareone Aikinheid xxv^{lib} xiiij^s Be
Doctour Burnett xx^{lib} Be Misteres Aikinheid xxx^{lib} vj^s Be
Jeane Alexander vj^{lib} xij^s Be Mistres Maill and hir anties
vij^{lib} xvij^c Be Colonell Hoome vj^{lib} xiij^s Be the Laird of Har-
tries xij^{lib} xij^s Mair be the said Mistres Maill iiij^{lib} ix^s Be Maister
Edward Keith iiij^{lib} iiij^s ij^d Be Gilbert Aitchiesone vj^{lib} xvj^s Item
moir be the said Walter Riddell by compt xix^{lib} xix^s Be the Lady
Comrie xv^s iiij^d Be Master Symontoune be compt iiij^{lib} Be
Rachaell Hope iij^{lib} xvij^s Be Daniell Clerk viij^{lib} ij^s Be the
Lady Rucksollis vij^{lib} Be the Laird of Troupe or Murrois xv^{lib}
vj^s 8^d Be Captane Ogilbie xij^{lib} xij^s Be the Laird of Kellie
iiij^{lib} viij^s Be the Laird of Rednoch and Maister James Keith his
cautioner xiij^{lib} xj^s viij^d Be Alexander Keith of Duffes xvj^{lib}
iiij^s Be Maister Alexander Forbes xxvij^{lib} Be Thomas Mylne
iij^{lib} iiij^s viij^d Be Johne Abircrombie x^{lib} iij^s Be Master Williame Spottiswood iiij^{lib} vij^s Be Johne Edmonstoune iiij^{lib} ij^s viij^d
Be the Lord Forbes ij^{lib} viij^s Be the Laird of Cluny younger
vj^{lib} Be Sir James Grahame xij^{lib} xij^s Be Thomas Steinsone
xviij^{lib} ij^s by two compts Be the Laird of Tilligony xvj^{lib} xvij^s Be
Rachaell Primrois lx^{lib} Be servitrix to Jonnet Foulles iij^{lib}
iiij^s Be Jonnet Forbes xviij^{lib} Be Maister James Thome xx^{lib}
Be Alexander Scattoune vij^{lib} Be James Riddell xxxvij^{lib} xvj^s Be
the tutour of Craigievar xxiiij^{lib} xij^s Be Mistres xxiiij^{lib} Be
Jonnet Prymrois v^{lib} xij^s Be Mistres Arnot xv^{lib} Be Mistres
Marie Chalmers xiij^{lib} Be Mistres Foulles v^{lib} Be the Laird of
Craigievar xiij^{lib} Be Monsiour Forbes j^{lib} vj^s Be Master James
Logan xiij^{lib} xiij^s Be the Lady Bonar viij^{lib} xvj^s Be Maister
James Keith be band of principall sowme bygane annualrent and
expensis iij^{c lib} Be Alexander Keith of principall sowme bygane
annualrent and expenssis j^c lx^{lib} Be Maister Symontoune for fur-
nysching xj^{lib} Be Alexander Forbes vij^{lib} or thairby Be Johne
Gordoune iiij^{lib} Be Maister James Balfour and his spous xxxviij^{lib}
vj^s Be Doctour Burnett xxxix^{lib} x^s Be Mistres Campbell x^{lib}
xiiij^s Be Maister James Balfour only restand of ane greater
sowme xliij^{lib} xviij^s Be Maister Furidell by compt iiij^{lib} ix^s Be
Mistres Dowglas v^{lib} Be Maister Sneddell iiij^{lib} xiij^s iiij^d Be the
Lady Bonners viij^{lib} viij^s Be James Riddell j^c xj^{lib} ij^s iiij^d Be

U

the Laird of Hartrie xxiiij^{lib} x^s Be Doctour Burnett xvij^{lib} iiij^s Be
Thomas Rob merchand in Edinburgh by band xix^{lib} x^s quhilk
band wes granted be him to Williame Burnett and assigned be
him to the said vmquhill   Be Adame Diksone in Niddrie
xxiij^{lib} Be Duncan Menzies of Comrie by ticket to the said
vmquhill Andro of xxx^{lib} Be the Lady Haystoune xxxiiij^{lib} Be
the Lady Forrester xlvij^{lib} ix^s Be Wmphra   vij^{lib} ix^s .
  Suma of the debts awine to the deid - ij^m xlj^{lib} 17^s viij^d
  Suma of the Inventar with the debts - ij^m ij^c lxxxj^{lib} 17^s 8^d
  No divisione.

Sir Johne Nisbitt &c. wndirstanding &c. we decerned &c. conforme to the quhilk &c. James Riddle merchand burges of Edinburgh cautioune as ane act beirs.

Commissariot
of Edinburgh.

Testaments.

Vol. 63.
8 January
1648.

Sir John Byres
of Coatts.

The Testament Dative and Inventar of the goods geir sowmes
of money and debts perteining to vmquhill Sir Johne Byris
of Coatts the tyme of his deceis quha deceist in the moneth
of   1648 yeirs ffaithfullie maid and givine vp be
Maister Robert Byres advocat tutour in law servit and
retourit to and in name and behalf of Johne Byris minor
sone lawfull to the said vmquhill Sir Johne Byris and onlie
Executor Dative decernit to him be decreit of the Commissars of Edinburgh as the saymne of the daitt the 8
day of December j^m vj^c fourtie sevine yeirs mair fullie
proports.

In the first the said vmquhill Sir Johne Byres had the goods
geir sowmes of money and debts of the availl and pryces efter-
following perteining to him the tyme of his deceis foirsaid Videlicet Imprimis four wark horssis estimat all to ij^c lxxx^{lib} Item
fourtie sex scheep estimat all to j^c lxxxiiij^{lib} Item growing wpone
the ground aucht bolls beir at vij^{lib} the boll fourtie bolls aitts at
sex pund the boll threttie bolls peis at fyve pund the boll suma of
the haill iiij^c xlvj^{lib} Item the straw of the foirsaid haill corne
estimat to iiij^c ^{lib} Item the insicht plennisching of his duellinghouse estimat to the sowme of j^m lib.
  Suma of the Inventar -   -   -   -   - ij^m iij^c x^{lib}

ffollowes the debts awine to the deid.

Item thair wes auchtand to the said vmquhill Sir Johne Byres the tyme of his deceis abonespecifeit Be Johne Denholme for heir ij^c xiij^{lib} vj^s viij^d Item be Thomas Forrest xl^{lib} Item be David Mowat xvj^{lib}

| Suma of the debts awine to the deid | ij^c lxix^{lib} vj^s viij^d |
| Suma of the Inventar with the debts | ij^m v^c lxxix^{lib} vj^s 8^d |

ffollowes the debts awine be the deid.

Item thair was auchtand be the said umquhill Sir Johne Byres to Maister James Crichtoune for ane half yeirs maill of his duelling hous in Edinburgh the sowme of j^c xiij^{lib} vj^s viij^d Item to Williame Samuell servand for his yeirs fie and bounteth lij^{lib} Item to Hew Jonstoune servand for his yeirs fie xx^{lib} vj^s Item to George Campbell servand for his yeirs fie xix^{lib} xvj^s Item to Johne Campbell for his yeirs fie twintie thrie pund   Item to Agnes Grosart servitrix for hir yeirs fie vij^{lib} x^s Item to Helene Cant servitrix for hir yeirs fie vij^{lib} x^s Item to Patrick Mairschell servand for his yeirs fie xvj^{lib} xiij^s iiij^d Item to Issobell Frame servitrix for hir yeirs fie xj^{lib} xvj^s Item to Maister Robert Hodge collectour of the moncthlie mantenance for thrie moneths mantenance preceiding the defunets deceis lxxxxv^{lib}

Suma of the debts awine be the deid	iiij^c iiij^{lib} xviij^s
Rests of frie geir the debts deducet -	ij^m j^c lxxiiij^{lib} viij^s 8^d
To be divydit in 3 pairts Deids	
pairt is - - - - -	vij^c xxiiij^{lib} xvj^s ij^d

Maisteris Johne Nisbett &c. understanding &c. we decernit conforme to the quhilk &c. Alexander Byres brother to the said Maister Robert become cautione as ane act beirs.

Edinburgh the xx day of October 1648.

Eik maid heirto as followes videlicet thair was justlie adebtit to the said defunct omittit out of his principall conformit Testament be his principall executour and now since the confirmatioune thairof is come to his knowledge videlicet thair is adebtit be Johne Bell in the Water of Leith the sowme of liiij^{lib} as the rest of his ferme crope and year of God 1646 quhilk being divydit in 3 pairts according to the divisione of the principall confirmit Testament deids pairt is xviij^{lib} Alexander Byres brother to the said Maister Robert become cautioune as ane act beirs.

TESTAMENT and INVENTORY of Mr. Thomas Byres, son
to the deceased John Byres of Coitts.

Commissariot
of Edinburgh.

Testaments.

Vol. 63.
29 November
1647.

Mr. Thomas
Byris, mer-
chant burgess
of Edinburgh.

The Testament Testamentar and Inventar of the goods geir
sownes of money and debts pertaining to vmquhill Maister
Thomas Byris sone lawfull to vmquhill Johne Byris of
Coitts merchand burges of Edinburgh the tyme of his
deceis Quha deceist in the moneth of   last
bypast 1647 yeirs ffaithfullie maid and givine up be himself
wpone the saxtene day of Junij the yeir of God foirsaid in
swa far as concernes the nominatioune of his executour
legacies and ane pairt of the debts auchtand be him and
givine vp be Maister Robert Byres advocat brother to the
defunct in swa far as concernes the haill Inventar of his
goods geir debts auchtand to him and maist pairt of the
debts auchtand be him quhome he nominat his onlie
Exectour in his Lattrewill wnderwrittin as the samyne of
the daitt foirsaid subscryvit with his hand in presens of
the witnessis eftirmentionat mair fullie proports.

In the first the said vmquhill Maister Thomas Byres had the
goods geir sownes of money and debts of the availl and pryces
eftirfollowing perteining to him the tyme of his deceis foirsaid
Videlicet Imprimis of silver wark ane maisser ane saltfatt twa
silver potts with covers twa porringers ellevine spoons four coupes
estimat all to iiijᶜ ᵗ Item in his duellinghouse ane chimney ane
pair of raxes and tanges estimat all to xvᵗᵇ twa panes ane pott and
ane speit estimat all to vjᵗᵇ Twa chandlers estimat baith to iiijᵗᵇ
Item ane round waunittrie buird with falling leivs estimat to
xxviijᵗᵇ Item ane fir buird estimat to iijᵗᵇ Item aucht chyres
and stools estimat to xxᵗᵇ Item four lethir chyres estimat all to
xyjᵗᵇ Item twa   of valnit trie estimat baith to xxxvjᵗᵇ
Item ane great walnit trie Frenche cabinet estimat to lᵗᵇ Item
ane littill sweit wood cabinet estimat to iiijᵗᵇ Item ane Frenche
coffer pryce thairof xijᵗᵇ Twa vther coffers estimat baith to xijᵗᵇ
Item ane resting chyre covered with Frenche schewing with ane
schewed cuscheone on the heid thairof estimat to xxxvjᵗᵇ Item
ane stand of arras hingings estimat to jᶜ lib Item ane stand of
Frenche   hinginges estimat all to xlviijᵗᵇ Item ane
stand of Taffeta courteins with ane pand of Damask with silk
freinezies with ane covering to ane chyre and ane table cloath
estimat all to jᶜ marks Item sax coverings to chyres schewed
with French schewing with silk freinezies estimate all to xxxvjᵗᵇ

Item ane fine capet cloath to the round boord estimat to xvj^{lib}
Item Frenche pand schewed to goe round about the bed estimat to
xx^{lib} Item ane littill cabinet covered with grein   and ane rid
lethir coffer estimat all to xvj^{lib} Item ane long greine tabill cloath
estimat to xij^{lib} Item twa fethir beds twa boustirs and four cods
estimat all to l^{lib} Item twa pair and ane single Spanische blankits
estimat to xxx^{lib} Item four pair of vther blankits and ane covering estimat all to xviij^{lib} Item ane pair of great and ane vther
pair of littill   estimat all to lx^{lib} Item ane Lint pryce thairof
xl^{lib} Item ane steikit tweill bed pryce thairof xviij^{lib} Item ane
dussane of dornick scrvitors and ane lairge tabill cloath estimat all
to xxiiij^{lib} Twa dussane of Frenche dornick servitouris and ane
lairge tabill cloath estimat all to xxiiij^{lib} Item twa dussane of
French dornick servitouris and twa buird cloaths estimat all to
xxxvj^{lib} Item ane dussane of blak silk servitouris estimat to v^{lib}
Item ane dussane of plaine lining serviters estimat all to vj^{lib}
Item ane dussane of hardine serviters estimat all to v^{lib} Item
fyve lining and harne buird cloaths estimat all to xv^{lib} Item ten
pair of scheits of lining and harne estimat all to xl^{lib} Item ane
littill schewed cabinet pryce thairof v^{lib} Item ane littill blak box
covered with black lethir pryce thairof iij^{lib} Item ane lairge
looking glas blak and covered pryce thairof xxx^{lib} Item ane littill
sweetwod looking glas pryce thairof iij^{lib} Item two chalmer potts
estimat both to xxx^s Item twelf plaitts estimat all to xvj^{lib} Item
ane quarter pynt choppine and mutchkine stoupes estimat all to
v^{lib} x^s Item of reddie gold and money lying besyde him the
sowme of iij^m iiij^c xxv^{lib} xij^s Item certane Frenche Latine and
Englische books estimat all to xx^{lib} Item the abulzements of his
bodie estimat to the sowme of j^c l^{lib}

Suma of the Inventar -   -   - iiij^m viij^c lxxij^{lib} v^s iiij^d

ffollowes the debts awine to the deid.

Item thair was auchtand to the said vmquhill Maister Thomas
Byres the tyme of his deceis abonespecifeit Be the Earle of
Siforth and his cautioneris to Issobell Conynghame relict of the
said vmquhill Maister Thomas and belonging to him jure mariti
the sowme of viij^m lib principall with vj^c xl^{lib} of byrune annualrent thairof Item be Sir David Crichtoune of Lugtoune and his
cautioneris to the said Issobell as perteining to him as said is the
sowme of ij^m ^{lib} principall with j^c lx^{lib} of byrune annualrent

thairof Item be the Earle of Dumfreis Lord Jonstoune and vthers to the said Issobell and perteining to him as said is the sowme of ij^m lib principall with j^c lx^lib of byrune annualrent thairof Item be the Earle of Dumfreis Lord Jonstoune and vthers to the said Issobell and perteining to him jure mariti as said is the sowme of ij^m lib principall with iiij^c xx^lib of byrune annualrent thairof Item be Thomas Somervell merchand burges of Edinburgh to the defunct and his said spous the sowme of iiij^c xiij^lib xiiij^s principall with xiij^lib of annualrent Mair be the said Sir David Crichtoune of Lugtoune ij^c lxvj^lib xiij^s iiij^d for the byrune annualrent of the principall sowme of fyve thousand marks adebtit be him conforme to his band Item thair auchtand to the said Issobell Conynghame as executrix confermit to hir vmquhill father Johne Conynghame and mentionat in the said vmquhill Johne his confermit Testament the compts reckoneing sowmes and vthers eftirspecifeit quhilkis pertenes to the said vmquhill Maister Thomas jure mariti videlicet Imprimis be James Somervell merchand in Edinburgh iij^c xxv^lib ix^s Item be Sir Johne Smyth as the remaines of ane compt j^c l^lib viij^s Item be James Boiswall merchand thair be compt ix^c l^lib ix^s quhairof ressavit twa hundereth dollers at fiftie four schillings the peice swa rests iiij^c x^lib ix^s Item be vmquhill Adame Rae burges of Edinburgh viij^c xlij^lib xij^s Item be Archbald Tod merchand thair j^c lxxxx^lib j^s viij^d Be vmquhill Johne Tuedie merchand vij^c lib vj^s viij^d Be Thomas Wilsoune youngar in Edinburgh ix^c xliiij^lib vj^s Be Thomas and James Somervells merchands j^m ix^c lxiiij^lib Be Johne Denholme merchand thair xj^c lxiij^lib xv^s Be Andro Rae induellar in Leith vj^c lxxij^lib xij^s Be Johne George merchand thair j^m x^lib x^s viij^d Be James Campbell merchand thair ix^c xiij^lib x^s Be the airs and executors of vmquhill Johne Grahame merchand thair viij^c lxxxxij^lib x^s ix^d Be Williame Patoune and Williame Stirling j^m lv^lib xix^s viij^d Be Johne Slowane merchand thair ij^c lxxxxix^lib xv^s Be Johne Denuistoune merchand viij^c lxxj^lib viij^d Be the airs and executours of vmquhill Williame Andersone in Pearth iiij^c xl^lib Be Thomas Hendersone merchand in Edinburgh iij^c l^lib xij^s Be Johne Schanks in Leith lxvj^lib xiij^s iiij^d Be Thomas Mudie merchand in Edinburgh iij^c xlviij^lib viij^s Be Gilbert Muire merchand thair v^c xj^lib viij^d Be James Campbell merchand thair j^c lib Be Androw Duncane merchand thair lx^lib Be Edward Sinclar sone to   Sinclar of Seba lxxxviij^lib Be the Committie of Estates vj^c lib principall

with ij^c xvj^{lib} for thrie yeirs annualrent thairof   Be Sir Williame
Gray the sowme of iij^m vj^c lxvj^{lib} xiij^s iiij^d principall with the
sowme of vj^c pundes of byrune annualrent thairof   Be Hew
Somervell and Elizabeth Somervell his spous the sowme of v^c ^{lib}
principall with lxxx^{lib} of byrune annualrent thairof   Be vmquhill
Maister Bartilmo Somervell the sowme of vj^m vj^c lxvj^{lib} xiij^s iiij^t

Suma of the debts awine to the deid xxxix^m ix^c lxvj^{lib} iij^s i^d
Suma of the Inventar with the
  debts   ·   ·   ·   ·   · lxiiij^m viij^c xxxviij^{lib} 8^s 5^d

ffollowes the debts awine be the deid.

Item thair wes auchtand be the said vmquhill Maister Thomas
Byres the time of his deceis foirsaid   To Alexander Byres merchand burges of Edinburgh his brother germane the sowme of
vij^c lib.

Suma of the debt awine be the deid   vij^c lib
Rests of frie geir the debts deducet   xliiij^m j^c xxxviij^{lib} 8^s 8^d
To be divydit in pairts   Deids
  pairt is ·   ·   ·   ·   ·

ffollowes the deids Legacie and Lattrewill.

Be it kend till all men be thir present Lettres   Me Maister
Thomas Byres sone laufull to vmquhill Johne Byres of Coitts
merchand burges of Edinburgh fforsameikill as I know myself to
be mortall and als being diseasit in bodie for the present and yet
perfyte in memorie and knowing nothing to be moir certane nor
death and nothing moir vncertaine thane the hour and tyme
thairof and being willing to put my earthlie affairs to ane poynt
that I may be the bettir prepared quhen it sall pleis God to call
me in mercie I mak my lattrewill and testament as followes   In
the first I leive my soull to God hopeing to be saved be the death
and merits of my Saviour Jesus Chryst and ordaines my bodie to
be bureid amongest the faithfull honnestlie as effeirs   And I have
nominat maid and constitute and be thir presents nominats makes
and constitutes my weelbeloved brother Maister Robert Byres my
brother germane my onlie executour sole legator and wniversall
intromettour with my haill goods geir and debts and lives and dis-
pones the samyne to him secluding all vtheiris thairfra   He
alwayes satisficing and paying my debts with power to him to give

vp Inventar thairof confirme Testament thairwpone and doe all
vther things requisit thairanent that of the law and consuetude of
this realme in sick caissis is knowine to perteane And because of
the great burdings and debts payit and vndertakine be me for my
belovit spous Issobell Conynghame as air to vmquhill Capitane
Johne Conynghame hir father I have not beine abill to fulfill to
my said spous hir contract of marriage Thairfor I heirby declair
that it is my will that immediatlie eftir my deceis schoe dispone
that pairt of the lands of Sauchtonhall and teinds thairof perteining to hir as air to hir said vmquhill father and als the lands and
tenements in Edinburgh to the best availl for payment of our
debts and burdinges quhairin I am ingadgit aither for myself or
for hir as air to hir father And to the effect the superplus thairof
may be imployit for implement of our contract of marriage for hir
lyfrent vse conforme to the tennour thairof and for payment and
satisfactione to James Conynghame hir vncle of that sowme of
provydit thairby to fall and belong to him in caice thair sall be no
bairnes procreat betwixt me and the said Issobell my spous in
caice the samyne be swa provydit be our contract of marriage conforme to the tennour thairof in all poynts And this I desyre to
be done and performit be my said spous as schoe wald deserve my
blissing And I declair that I am adebtit and auchtand to Alexander Byres my brother germane the sowme of vij^c lib money
quhairfor he hes no band nor ticket of me and quhich I have
givine ordour to my said spous to cause be payit freith of thais
moneyis lying besyde me In witnes quhairof I have subscryvit
with my hand thir presents writtin be Maister James Cheyne
wryter at Edinburgh the saxtene day of Junij 1647 yeirs befor thir
witnessis Maister James Rid minister of God's word at S^t. Cuthberts Kirk neir Edinburgh the said Maister James Cheyne and
Johne Craufurd servitour to the said Maister James Rid It is
alwayse declairit that in caice it sall happine my said spous to be
with chyld and the said chyld to come to perfectione that thane
and in that caice thir presents sall be null and the said office of
executrie with my saids goods and geir to belong to my said chyld
and my said executour to be secludit thairfra siclyk and in the
samyne maner as gife thir presents had never bene maid nor subscryvit Sic subscribitur Mr Thomas Byres Mr. James Reid witnes
Jo^n Craufurd witnes.

Maisteris Johne Nisbitt   Ratifies and approves   and gives

and committs   Reservand compt   Alexander Byres brother
to the said Maister Robert Byres became cautioune as ane act
beirs.

---

4 September 1621. Sasine on Charter by Isabell Dalzell, daughter
of the late James Dalzell, burgess of Edin^r, in favour of John
Byres of Coittis, merchant burgess of Edinburgh, of the Kirk-
lands and glebe of St. Cuthberts, with the barn, grange, grass
yard, &c., situated under the castle wall of Edinburgh, on the east
side of the cemetery. Richard Byres, miller, burgess of Edin-
burgh, is a witness. See p. 103. Particular Register of Sasines, Edinburgh. Vol. V., fol. 25.

6 November 1622. Sasine on Charter by Alexander Logan,
burgess of Edin^r, to John Byres, portioner of Coittis, of portions
of the lands of Brochtoun, in the regality and barony thereof,
and shire of Edinburgh. Vol. VII., fol. 44.

28 June 1623. Sasine on Charter by Mr. Patrick Hepburn, of
Smetoun, and Marion Adamson, his spouse, to John Byres, of
Coittis, and Agnes Smyth, his spouse, of an annuity of 400 merks,
out of the mains of Smetoun, in the shire of Haddington. Vol. VIII., fol. 25.

10 November 1624. Sasine on Charter by Mr. Samuel Gray,
advocate, and Jean Kincaid, his mother, to John Byres, of Coittis,
Dean of Gild of Edinburgh, of an annual rent of 200 merks, out
of certain lands which belonged to the late James Kincaid of
Coittis. Vol. IX., fol. 292.

31 January 1625. Sasine on Charter by John Ormistoun to
John Byres, of Coittis, merchant burgess of Edinburgh, of two
acres of the lands of Coittis. Vol. X., fol. 29.

2 July 1625. Sasine on Charter by Mr. Samuel Gray, advocate, to John Byres, of Coittis Dean of Gild of Edin^r, of 200
merks yearly, out of certain acres of the Coittis. Vol. X., fol. 159.

20 July 1625. Sasine on Charter by John Lord Holyrood- Vol. X., fol. 299.

house to John Byres, of Coittis, Dean of Guild of Edinburgh, in life rent, and John B., his eldest son, in fee, of an annual rent of 200 merks out of the teinds of St. Cuthberts.

29 Dec. 1625. Sasine on Charter by David Crichtoun, junior, of Lugtoun, to John Byres, merchant burgess of Edinburgh, and Agnes Smyth, his wife, in life rent, and Thomas, Alexander, and Janet Byres, their children, of the sunny half of the lands of St. Leonard's, near Edinburgh. One of the witnesses is James Byres, servitor to said John B., of Coittis.

9 January 1626. Reversion by the sᵈ John Byres, of Coittis, to sᵈ D. Crichtoun over the lands of St. Leonard's for 5000 merks.

25 April 1627. Sasine on Charter by Robert Scot, eldest son of the late Alex. Scott, of Orchardfield, to John Byres, of Coittis, of certain acres of the Coittis.

2 June 1627. Renunciation by John Byres, of Coittis, to Mr. Samuel Gray of an annual rent of 200 merks.

4 July 1628. Sasine on Charter by Mr. Samuel Gray, advocate, and Katherine Lockhart, his wife, to John Byres, of Coittis, and Agnes Smyth, his wife, in life rent, and John Byres, their son, in fee, of certain acres of the Coittis.

4 July 1628. Sasine on Charter by John Byres, of Coittis, merchant burgess of Edinburgh, to Agnes Smyth, his spouse, in life rent, of seven acres, called the Howpairt of Coittis, and seven acres of Coittis lying contiguous under the Bourtriebus, which lands, with the sum of 5000 merks, were laid out upon the sunny half of the lands of St. Leonard's, with mansion house, &c., near the burgh of Edinburgh, in the regality and barony of Brochtoun, in favour of his said spouse in life rent, in implement of their marriage contract, to which Robert Smyth, merchant burgess of Edinburgh, and the late Agnes Purves, his spouse, parents of said Agnes Smyth, were parties.

REGISTER OF DEEDS.

Date of Registration.

1618. April 16. Michael Byres, burgess of Hamilton, gets Vol. 271.
obligation from Archibald Hamilton, of Marritoun, and Jean Weir
his spouse, in favour of said Michael, and Michael his son, for 112
merks, dated at Hamilton, 10. March 1603. One of the witnesses
is James Byres, burgess of Hamilton.

1619. 26. Jany. Obligation by Robert Loch, in Birdsfield, to Vol. 279.
Michael Byres, burgess of Hamilton, for 160 merks, dated 30.
Jany. 1613.

1620. 1ˢᵗ Augᵗ Obligation by Robert Byres, younger, merchant, Vol. 297.
son of the late James Byres, indweller in Hamilton, to William
Gairdin, burgess of Edinburgh, for £160 scots., dated at Louden-
dean, 24. Feby. 1620.

1622. 15. May. Obligation by John Somerville, younger of Vol. 318.
Cambusnethane, to Michael Byres, burgess of Hamilton, for 860
merks, dated at Hamilton 22. July 1618. This deed is written by
Mr William Byres, servant to John Byres, merchant-burgess of
Edinburgh.

1622. Decʳ 11. Obligation by Thomas Waugh in Decmont Vol. 332.
(West Lothian), to Thomas Byres, in Scarlaw, for 100 merks, dated
at Linlithgow, 1. Decʳ 1621.

1623. 7. Augᵗ Obligation by James Fergushill, merchant-bur- Vol. 346.
gess of Ayr, to James Byres, in Ardgowan, see p. 98, for 200 merks.
19. May 1620.

1624. 16. June. Obligation by John Hamilton, burgess of Vol. 359.
Hamilton, to Michael Byres, burgess of Hamilton, for 100 merks,
dated at Hamilton, 14. June 1612.

PARTICULAR SASINES OF EDINBURGH.

Vol. 16.
Fol. 312.

1630. Novr 2. Sasine to "a discreet young man," John Byres, son and heir of the late John Byres of Coates, proceeding upon a precepit of clare constat for infeifting the said John, as heir to his father, in half of the lands of Coates, with mansion houses, &c., formerly belonging to Clement Kincaid, of Coates, in the barony and regality of Broughton, and shire of Edinburgh. John Smyth, merchant-burgess of Edinburgh—probably his uncle—his attorney (the different parts of estates are mentioned). Witnesses, Thomas Charteris, Alexander Heriot, merchant-burgesses of Edinburgh, and James Byres, servant to the late John Byres.

Vol. 17.

1631. May 2. Sasine proceeding on charter granted by Alexander Heriot, merchant-burgess of Edinburgn, in favour of Margaret Byres, his wife, of twelve acres of the lands of Bonnington, and part of the lands of Hillhousefield (both in Midlothian).

Vol. 19.
Fol. 201.

1632. July 30. Sasine proceeding upon a charter by John Lord Holyroodhouse, in favour of John Byres, son and heir of the late John Byres of Coates, of the teinds of the parish of St. Cuthbert's, under the Castle wall. Charter dated at Holyroodhouse, 10. April 1631, one witness being James Cairns, servitor to Agnes Smyth, relict of the deceased John Byres. The baillie, that is, the person who acts for him, is James Byres, servitor to Agnes Smyth, relict of the said John Byres.

EDINBURGH SASINES.

Vol. 28.
Fol. 58.

1639. March 29. Sasine proceeding upon charter by Thomas Kincaid of Warrestone, to Mr John Byres, his heirs and assignees heritably, of all and whole those 26 acres of arable land of the Coates, with mansion houses, buildings, &c., Kincaid being superior. Charter dated at Edinburgh, 3^d Octr 1638.

1640. May 7. Sasine proceeding upon charter by Thomas Fol. 412. Kincaid of Warrestone, in favour of Mr John Byres of Coates, of the lands of Warrestone. In this document Elizabeth Byres is mentioned as the first wife of Thomas Kincaid, elder, and the mother of Thomas Kincaid, younger.

1642. June. 2. Bond by Sir David Crichton of Lugton, Knight, Vol. 30. to Mr Thomas and Alexander Byres, lawful sons of the late John Fol. 164. Byres of Coates, for £1,000, referring to another bond of date 15. Septr 1625, by the late David Crichton of Lugton, to the said late John Byres of Coates, and Agnes Smyth his wife, for 10,000 merks. This bond is dated at Edinbro', 1st June 1642.

1642. 2. June. Bond by said Sir David Crichton to Mr Robert Fol. 165. Byres, lawful son of the late John Byres of Coates, for £1,000. Given in security for it, the lands of St. Leonard's.

1643. May 27. Sasine proceeding upon charter granted by the Vol. 31. Provest, Baillies, and Ministers of the town of Edinburgh, as Fol. 222. Governors of Heriot's Hospital, and superiors of the town of Broughton, and Canonmills, in favour of Sir John Byres of Coates, Knight, of various portions of the lands of Coates, Whinnie Knowes, and others, in the barony and regality of Broughton, and also the lands of Warristone. In this document the first wife of Thomas Kincaid is called Elizabeth *Burrell*, not Byres; see above. Witnesses to Sasine, John and William Byres, residing at the Water of Leith. See p. 110.

Sasine proceeding on charter by Sir David Crichton of Lugton, Vol. 31. superior, in favour of Mr Robert, and Mr Thomas, and Alexander Fol. 270. Byres, lawful sons of the late John Byres of Coates, begotten between him and Agnes Smyth his spouse, equally between them, of the half lands of St. Leonards, and mansion houses, &c., reserving to the said Agnes Smyth her conjunct fee of the said sunny half of the lands of St. Leonards.

1643. June 24. Sasine proceeding upon precept granted by Sir Fol. 272. David Crichton in favour of Sir John Byres, of the half of the lands of St. Leonards. Mr Robert Byres acts as attorney for said Sir John.

WILL OF ROBERT BYRES OF DUBLIN.

In the name of God Amen. I Robert Byres of the City of Dublin merchant being in perfect health of body and in sound mind and memory designeing to goe to Scotland make this my last will and testament in manner following Imprimis I comit my soul to Almighty God who gave it me hopeing through the merritts death and passion of Jesus Christ I shall obtain everlasting salvation, and as to my worldly goods and chattells debts credits and estate whatsoever reall or personall with which it hath pleased God to bless me I dispose of the same in manner following Imprimis I order that all my debts which shall be due by me att the time of my death be paid out of the first and readiest of my estate Next I leave and bequeath to my dearest spouse besides and above the benefit of our Martrimoniall Contract two hundred and fiftie pounds sterling at her own disposall provided she dye my widow and the annual Rent and Interest of said mony dureing her viddowhood and no longer and if she marry or dye Intestate I leave and bequeath the said two hundred and fiftie pounds equally amongst the children begotten or to be begotten betwixt us and also I bequeath to my daughter Jean Two hundred and ffiftie pounds sterling two thirds to be paid att her marriage vith her mothers or my exers in trust their consent and one third at her mother's death and if I have another child male or femalle before or after my death I leave and bequeath the like portion of Two hundred and Fiftie pounds sterling to be paid in like manner to the said child Alsoe I leave and bequeath to James Byres my nephew and apprintice two hundred pounds two thirds of it at ye Expiration of his apprintiship one third att my wiffes death. Alsoe I leave to Robert Souper my nephew fiiftie pounds sterling to be 1^d at my death and the like summ of Fiftie pounds ster to George Sandilands my brother in law whom I appoint my trustie for settling my affairs in Ireland and sending my family and remitting all my efiects to my Exers Trusties in Scotland hereafter named I likewise leave the said Geo Sandilands Sixty pounds per annum occasioned by my business for his personall charges and trouble in ending my business in Irland besides the necessary occasioned by my business untill my Trusties in Scotland discharge his further attendance leaving my said Trusties full power to discharge him and appoynt another at their pleasure ; and as to all my other debts and credits

Goods and Estate reall and personall in Kingdome of Great Brittain and Ireland or elsewhere I leave and devise the same to James Byres my onely sone and failling him to any other sone that I may have afterwards, failling which to be equally divided amongst my daughters if I have more than one at the time of my death and if but one to her and failing issue of my own body instead of the Fiftie pounds forementioned I leave one hundred pounds to the said George Sandilands fiftie pounds to his brother William Sandilands, one hundred pounds to my nephew Robert Souper and Fiftie pounds to every childe sone or daughter that either of my sisters vizt Jean wiffe to William Souper of Aberdeen and Isabell wife of Robert Gordon of Burdeaux merchant now have or shall have to be paid att their marriage with their parents' consent or at their comeing to the age of Twenty one years and all the Rest of my Estate Reall and Personall I leave to the said James Byres my nephew. Item I appoint James Moire Esqre of Stonywood, Mr Alex^t Thomson Town Clerk of Aberdeen, Patrick Sandilands younger of Cotton, and the said William Souper to be my executors in Trust to see my effects setled for the foresaid uses and leave them or any two of them full power to mannage all my affairs untill my children or other air come to age and to give them what part of what I now leave and bequeath they shall think fitt before they come to age. I order the necessary charges alliment and education of my younger children to be born and p^d out of my eldest sones legacye desireing I may be decently and frugally enterred, and I hereby revoke and make void all other and former wills by me made and publish this my last will and testament As witness my hand and seall this Sixth day of May One thousand seven hundred and twelve.

Signed sealed and published in presence of us the words " and Irland " and the word divided being first interlined.

(Sig^d) ROBERT BYRES.

  (Sig^d) PATRICK MITCHELL. GEORGE SANDRY.
   ,,   WALT^R ROBERTSON.

ACCOUNT PAID OUT BY WILLIAM SOUPER FOR
ALEX⁸ HAY OF ARNBATH.

P'd	To what I payed the Lady Arnbath - -	109 16 0
P'd	To what I payed John Thain by Stoniwood's order - - - - -	110 5 0
P'd	To Alexʳ Invine of Safoch as p receipt -	139 16 0
P'd	To Charles Stuart in Cullen - -	173 6 8
P'd	To John Forbes of Balflig - -	333 6 8
P'd	To Culwhick by Stoniwood's order -	333 6 8
P'd	To George Keith as p his bill - -	51 7 10
P'd	To the Lady Arnbath - - -	66 13 8
P'd	To Mr. Archibald Dumbar as p bill -	360 0 0
P'd	To Patrick Gellie as p his dicharge -	733 6 8
P'd	To Balie Catanach as p bond & interest and expences - - - -	635 6 0
P'd	To the Litsters hoypital prinp. and interest till Whitsunday 1720 being 2½ years -	225 0 0
P'd	To Mʳ Patrick Coupland Minister of Tuch	540 0 0
P'd	To Mʳ George Keith - - -	800 0 0
P'd	To William Simson - - -	192 0 0
P'd	To John Innes Colquhich - -	25 0 0
P'd	To Mʳ James Chalmers Minister at Dyke	575 0 0
P'd	To Alexʳ Watson - - -	80 0 0
P'd	To James Udny - - -	182 0 0
P'd	Mʳ Alexʳ Thomson p bond - -	240 0 0
P'd	To Alexʳ Thomson p two bills - -	1012 10 0
P'd	To Stoniwood & Licklyhead of rent -	62 10 0
P'd	To Patrick Byres - - -	2723 6 8
	To Ditto - - -	2200 0 0
P'd	To Alexʳ Leslie in Kintore - -	450 0 0

12353 16 10

Summa is Twelve thousand three hundred fifty three pounds sixteen shillings ten pennies Scots money qh shall be allowed for part of the paymt of the lands of Tonley by Alexʳ Hay.

Abdn 25 June 1720.

Transferred from the preceding page -	£12,353	16	10
It. to Portlethen per Aranbaths bond -	- 473	17	0
Item to Misstress Thomson in Old Aberdeen	- 375	0	0
Item to Stonnywood - - -	- 1,846	10	2
Item to the Relict of the Minister of Tuch -	- 266	13	4
Item to Rothney - - - -	- 200	0	0
Item to Alexʳ Thomson - - -	- 20	15	10
Item to the Lady Ardinbath - -	- 266	13	4
Item payed to William Souper - -	- 7	10	0
Item for registratione of the renonciatione -	- 5	6	8
Item to the Minister of Mortleth - -	- 800	0	0
Item to Mʳ George Keith - - -	- 80	0	0
Summa is - - -	£16,696	3	2
Price of the lands - -	16,666	13	4
Ballance to be payed by Stonnywood	- £29	9	10

The above is in full and compleit payment and satisfactione of the price of the lands of Tonley and others disponed by Alexʳ Hay of Ardinbath and Clinshaw Aberdeen To Patrick Byres only son and child to the deceased Robert Byres merchant in Dublin In witness whereof the said Alexʳ Hay has subscribed these presents at Aberdeen the twenty seventh day of June One thousand seven hundred and twenty years before these witnesses Walter Hay of Lickleyhead and Alexʳ Thomson writter in old Aberdeen writter hereof

ALEXʳ HAY.

COPIED from ORIGINAL LETTERS bound into the Stoney-wood MS., in the possession of W. F. SKENE, W.S., whose father compiled it. No. 158. (Marked "from Capt Byres.")

I.—LETTER, Patrick Byres, of Tonley, dated from Duffus, to Collo James Moir, of Stoneywood, att Findhorn, 1746, 18 March.

1746.

" Dʳ Sir,—Before I coud dispatch the Carts and the Horses into Elgin Mʳ Moir arrived here, and told me you was marchᵈ wᵗ a

Y

part of the Battalion for findhorn, and proposed that I should meet you on the West road from Elgin. As its impossible for me to bring the men to findhorn to-night, having sent them into Elgin w^t the carts, I thought proper to send the bearer to know if I should join you to-morrow there, or continue the party at Gordonston till furder orders. If I be to join you at ffindhorn you'll please caw^d (caused) Raeburn goe directly from you to Elgin, and cause the Lieutennatt or Ensign bring them up there, and then come to me here, but if the party be to be continued at Gordonstin he may come straight here, and I shall bring them out here. I ever. Yrs &^{c}

(Signed)   "Pat^k Byres."

1747.   II.—Letter, No. 164.—From last, addressed A. Mons. Monsieur Jacques Jameson (Stoneywood's assumed name, and a ready description of his parentage, James, son of James), Negociant, a Gottenburgh, dans la Suede, dated Paris 18 May 1747.

" Sir,—Some days ago I received yours of the 18th ultimo O.S. Since my last to you the prince is returned from M—d, and lives at present in a village called Pessy, about a league from here. In consequence of yours I went there, and communicate yours to Sir Jo. Graham, who told me what I knew very well before, viz., that though the Court of France had approved of the list you and I were in, and had ordered the pay^t y^{r}of, and altho' on the faith of that Mr Waters had advanced above 4000 Livres, yet as the demands for the campagne had been, and still continued very pressing, the Intendent of the ffinances had not as yet pay^d in any part of the money ordered by that list of Mr Waters, and that till it was pass^d he would advance no more, but that he had writt to the —— Minister the very day I spoke to him, and that he Expected the money would be very soon pay^d in to Waters. That how soon that happened, he'd let me know, and I should have ane order for yours and y^r broyr's. As I know very well that every word of the above was true I could say nothing in return ; only I told him that as I had writt you in Consequence of his own desire, I wish^d he^d give me ane order on Waters. He said he would willingly, but he was sure Waters would not pay it (having refused severalls before) till he was reimburs'd of his advance, which could not be long. I likewise ment^d you and Charlie to the Prince at dinner, who expressed his satisfaction of your being safe, and seem'd very well pleased when I told him that you'd be in Scotland among the first of his friends. When that will be God knows, tho' we hope here it won't be long. Please make my compliments to Messrs. Scot and Carnegie, and tell them they ere in the same list with us, and will draw 1000 Livres each when the money is pay⁴, being insert as Captains. Sir James Stewart and his family have been at S⁺ Seden since November last, S⁺ James Leslie is w⁺ the army in Flanders, Lochell is and has been here since the p⁺ (Prince) arrived. I beg you'll make my compliments in every particular way to M⁺ Baxter, and tell him when he goes home I hope he'll be so good as lett my wife and the rest of my friends know I am well, for tho' I have writt severall times, yett as the communication to Holland is now stop⁺, I doubt very much if we can expect to hear from Britt. by that way, and let me know if you think it more praciticable y⁺ way. As to business, there is scarce any possibility of success here ; the war has ruined that at present. So that the army is the only rescource at present which I am not as yet determined to follow. Shall be glad to know what scheme youre on, and how you propose to prosecute it. Severall British letters insist positively that there is to be a second bill of attainder. The F. are carrying all before them in Dutch Flanders: they have taken Sluice, Sas de Grand, fort Phillyspinee and Hulst, but have lost a considerable number of men before Hulst, the dutch having defended it better than their o'yr towns since the Election of a Stadhoulder. We expect daily the news of a generall action in flanders, which is thought unavoidable, and if the Allies be beat Its hard to foresee what may be the consequence. The D——ke has left this some time ago privately and where's he gone is a secret. remember me to young Gask, and to honest Generall Gordon. We drink all your healths often. L⁴ Lewis is on this this side the water, S⁺ Will Gordon is here, and is L. Coll. to L⁴ Ogil.—I am, Sir, Y⁺ Most Humbl⁰ Servent,

(Sig⁴)   " PAT. BYRES.

" P.S.—When I write to Scotland I sign Pat Robertson, but there's no danger twixt this and you I sign my own name."

III.—LETTER, No. 189.—From last to same, dated Paris, 10 Aprile 1747 N.S.

" Sir,—I received yours of the 7ᵗʰ ulto.—I suppose old style—

some days ago, though I have reasons enough to excuse my
declining any correspondence w^t you, after the usage I very un-
deservedly met w^t from you, whereof, though you make no mention, I make no doubt of youre being sensible, yet, as it was
always my principall that of the two I'd rather any man were in
the wrong to me than I to him, I therefor thought it incumbent
on me to acquaint you of some facts which concern you. You
must know then that after being some time here, on hearing that
your Brother and you were arrived at Gotheburg, as there was a
list of the prince's friends making up, in order to be given in to the
Court of france, I waited on Sir Jo. Graham, who does business here
for the Duke of York, and told him that your Broy^r and you were
arrived in Sweden, and desired that he would put you in the List,
which he was making up of the prince's friends. He ask'd what
Quality you had serv'd in. I told him you as Coll. and your
broy^r as Capt of Lord L. Gordon's first Batt. He said he would
insert you as Lt Coll. and your Broy^r as Capt, seeing he knew
that you had acted as such, Ld Lewis having been Coll. himself,
which was accordingly done ; and now the Court of ffrance have
issued the money for the payment of that List, so that there's
1500 livres for you and 1000 for Charlie, which you and he may
send orders to any one of your friends here to wait on Sir Jo.
Graham, who will give any one so Impower'd ane order on M^r
Waters, the Banq^r, for each of these sums. You^{ll} need also, I
believe, send at same time y^r recepts to Mr Waters for his ex-
oneration in case you propose to draw the money, and directions
What way to apply or remitt it after Mr Waters pays it. I believe
the Court of france may be prevail'd on to make some more
pay^{ts} in the same way to such of the prince's friends as are not as
yett oyrwise provided for, though I doubt much of their being
continue^d. I have writt to Scotland to let Charlie know of this,
in case he should be still there. I am heartily Concern'd I do
assure you for thi loss you have suffered in your family by the
death of your two sons. If Charlie come to Sweden I'm still of
opinion that he could do better here than anywhere else. However, as his best judge of that is himself, I only hint it that he
may have it in his eye. Mr Ogilvie, of Inshewan, who is just now
w^t me, desires to be remembered to you.—I am, Sir, Your Most
Humble Servant,

(Sig^d) " PAT. BYRES.

" P.S.—I desire that Charlie may write me how soon he arrives in Sweden, and if you write to Scotland that you'd fall on some way to cause him Write me from there if he has not yett left the country."

IV. LETTER, No. 190—Patrick Byres to James Moir, Paris, 1st August 1747.

"Sir,—At last, after being obliged to be severall times at the trouble to go and come to the prince's Quarters at St Toin, which is 2 leagues from here, I Got an order from Sr Jo. Graham on Mr Waters for 1500 livres for you, and enoyr for 1000 for Charlie, and on giving my recept on the back of them Mr Waters has payd me the money, which is now in my custody. I was obliged to leave your orders wt Sir Jo. as a voucher to him before he'd Give me a precept on Mr Waters, so on recept of this, youll send me a recept for the 1500 Livres, as mine lyes wt Mr Waters, and in the meantime I shall endeavour to gett a Bill for said sum on Holland payable to Mr Crawford, tho' I could wish to hear from you first, as possibly you may have altered your intention, it has cost me about five and twenty or thirty livres in Coach hire, &c., solliciting for you, which I suppose you will not grudge. We have had here Copies of ane act of the British parlt which they pretend to dignifie wt the title of a Bill of Indemnity, tho' in my opinion, it ought rather to be call'd a 2d Bill of Attaindre. There are in it 85 Gentlemen Excepted, besides those already attainted, of wh number yr unkle, you, and I are three. Besides these 85 Excepted by name, all abroad, all in foreign service, all transported, and all any manner of way concerned in the late rebellion are excepted in one Generall Clause, so that one or oyr Everybody is Included; tho' as to those not Excepted by name, in my opinion I think they may wtout any danger go home —and I was resolved to have done so myself had I not been Excepted. I had a letter from Robie Sandilands two or three posts ago, to which I wrote him ane answer the 23d ulto wt my thoughts anent what he should do, which I see no reasons hitherto to alter. Please remember me to him, and tell him that I have gott him mark'd down as a Capt in a list they are just now making up to be given in to the Court, but when it will be given in or when pay'd is very uncertain. Had he write a post sooner he had been in a list just now given in, and which will, I believe, be soon pay'd. He wrote me your Lady was come over, I hope she

is well ; please remember me to her. The only news here are
that the french have been sadly defeat in Italy, and have lost yor
8000 men and a number of Generall offr^s ; out of 28 Battⁿ there
are 27 Collonels slain along with the Chev^{lr} de Belisle who commanded that Corps, and is said the Marschall de Belisle and the
whole army have retired to the frontiers of provence, which if
true, is a very great check. Glenbuckett arrived here two or
three Days ago w^t Mr Menzies. In order to save postage I have
writt Charlie on this. Having nothing further to add.—I am, Sir,
Your Most Humble servant,

(Sig^d)   " PAT. BYRES."

V. LETTER, No. 191—Patrick Byres to Mr Charles Moir.

" PARIS, 1st August 1747.

" Dear Charlie,—I had your's from Gotthburgh, and was glad
to   you had got safe. I have gott your 1000 livres, and
shall remitt or employ it as you order; in my opinion you should
come here, as your passage to Holland would cost you nothing.
Tarriebreecks you know pay^t no freight, and when in Holland
you should gett your self made Burger at Rott^{dm}, and then pro-
ceed to Ostend, Dunkerque, or any oyr place of that kind, and
buy a prize which you know you can do pretty easy, and so youll
be just in your old way again, and might be usefull to y^r friends.
Your being made burger at Rott^{dm} will cost you but a triffle of 15
or 20f, or if you please you may gett your self made a Burger of
Gottenburgh, which I believe would be better, and then you
could sail your vessell as a Swedish ship, for in all probebility the
Dutch will soon be in war w^t the french. This is my scheme,
but if you have any better of your own you know Counsel's not
Command. When you write me how to order your 1000 livres,
send on a recept along because mine lyes for it. I heard lately
from y^r aunt all is well at home, and she writes me that you had
left Scotland sometime ago. Make my compliments to all friends,
and I ever am, Dear Charlie, Yours Most affectionatly,

(Sig^d)   "While PAT. BYRES."

To Mr Charles Moir.

DUEL between JOHN LEITH of Leith-hall and JAMES
ABERNETHY of Mayen, 1763.

"Archibald Campbell's House," stood on the site now occupied
by the premises of the North of Scotland Banking Company, and
was a well-known place of festive entertainment in the City of
Bon-Accord a hundred years ago. It was in that house, subsequently known as "The New Inn," about or soon after midnight
of 21ˢᵗ December 1763—at which season, in consequence of the
20ᵗʰ December being held, in that part of Scotland, as one of the
half-yearly money terms, many gentlemen from the country dis-
tricts visit Aberdeen—that, in the progress of a convivial meeting,
a quarrel arose between John Leith of Leith-hall and James Abernethy of Mayen in Devronside; which, from its fatal termination,
attracted at the time considerable public attention, and was comme-
morated in a ballad still remembered in some parts of the country.
The origin of the dispute seems to have been forgotten, but the
party then assembled had evidently entertained no apprehension
of its terminating disastrously, as on the two disputants leaving
the room the only remark which seemed to have been made was
by one of the gentlemen still remaining in the apartment, who
casually observed that "Leith would take care to keep out of
harm's way." In a short time, the sound of firearms out of doors
having been heard, the portion of the company that had remained
at table rushed out to ascertain the cause, when Leith-hall was
found lying on the plain-stanes, nearly opposite to Archibald
Campbell's house, wounded (and, as it soon proved, mortally), by
a pistol bullet in his forehead. The unhappy gentleman died on
the third day thereafter. His adversary, reported to have been
slightly wounded on the thigh, evaded justice by immediate flight
to the Continent. It is said that one of the balls fired on the
occasion was to be seen for many years sticking in a neighbouring
lamp post.—(The Book of Bon-Accord, 1839, p. 156.)

In reference to that occurrence, the Editor of the Black
Kalendar of Aberdeen (Edition 1840, p. 77), observes:—"It has
been stated, though we do not place unhesitating reliance on the
story, that the quarrel between Leith-hall and Mayen might have
been settled but for the interference of Patrick Byres of Tonley,
who urged Mayen to the deed, and even loaded his pistol. It is

certain that he left the country along with Mayen." Mr Abernethy was indicted to stand trial at the Circuit Court of Justiciary,
held at Aberdeen in May 1764, before Lord Auchinleck. In the
Scots Magazine for 1764, it is recorded that, "At Aberdeen,
James Abernethy of Mayen, Esq., was outlawed, for not appear-
ing to stand trial on an indictment for the murder of John Leith
of Leith-hall, Esq."

Memoir of
James Young,
&c., by the
late A. John-
ston, W.S.

"The late Dr James Moir of Aberdeen gives a different account
of the nature of his grandfather's (Patrick Byres) interference on
the occasion referred to. The Doctor relates that it is true that
Tonley was of the party whereat the dispute happened between
Leith-hall and Mayen; and that Patrick Byres followed them
when they left Archibald Campbell's house, but that before M^r
Byres had reached the plain stanes, Leith-hall had been wounded,
after which Mr Byres procured horses for his wife's nephew in
order to enable the latter to escape from the town."

From a verse of a local ballad commemorating this sad event, it
is evident that the feeling in the country at the time was against
Mayen.

> " The brave Leith-hall went down the stair,
> Not knowing what to do,
> The cruel men they followed him,
> And shot him through the broo" (brow).

LETTER.—JA^s MONTGOMERIE, Elgin, to ALEX^r DUNBAR, Esq.,
Student of Law, Edinburgh.

8. *Feby.* 1764.

"Sir,— At the desire of your friend the old Lady, I trouble you
with the enclosed to which please to be refer'd as Mr Riddoch is
a very dilitary sort of man. She not only insists for your own good
offices but that you will likewise be a spur to him, who can inform
you fully of the affair. The Laird takes a particular concern in
this, of which he desired you might be acquainted, and that he
will expect a proper account of your Progress, &c. &c.

Nothing new in this corner, Mayen and Leithhall's story has
occasioned much speculation of late, the Laird (Archibald Dunbar
of Thunderton), invariably exposes Mayen's side, and swears

that in the first place Mayen is a gentleman, secondly a Brave man, and lastly that their Grandmothers were sisters (see p. 82). Consequently quite incapable of doing anything base.

(Sign^d)   " Ja^s Montgomerie."

EXTRACT LETTER.—John Leslie, King's Coll., Aberdeen, to Archibald Dunbar, Esqr^e of Thunderton, at Duffus.

9th Feby. 1764.

" Your son tells me you are anxious to have some account of Leithhall's death.

"There is such a variety of contradictory stories about that affair, that one does not know what to write. It is not generally agreed that Mr Byres is perfectly innocent, and it is said that all Leithhall's friends except Blackhall, are willing to drop the prosecution against him.

"It is likewise said that great interest will be used for a pardon to Mayen, in case it shall appear to have been a duel."

LETTER from Pat. Duff, Elgin, to Archibald Dunbar, Esqre., of Newton.

27. Decr. 1763.

" Sir,—I dont wonder that you and every gentleman feels for the family of the unhappy gentleman at Aberdeen. The way it rose I hear is, that they and some others had been drinking all night. That Leithhall, Mayen, and Byres, about four in the morning came to the Street in a ffriendly way. Leithhall having ordered his servt. to put on a fire to him in his room, and for ought yet known here suspected no Damage. Mayen to resent an old quarrel, privatly desired his ser^t to go for his pistols, they were accordingly brought, whether any information was given to Leithhall I have not yet learned, but so it is he was shot as in my last. His Ser^t heard the report and being alarmed thereby run to the Street found his master lying and this Byres by him. He apprehended Byre, and while he held him Byre called on Mayen to return and shoot the ser^t with his oy^r pistol as he had done his master, the ser^t cried out for help and Byres was keept. Mayen broke open the stable door, took out his horse and rode of without obots or Big Coat. Poor Leithhall ffevered Saturday and died on

Z

Sunday morning. This came last night or this morning p' express. His Lady on her arrival was not permitted to speak to him being then speechless. I am going throw your processes, but to write of them sensibly will take sometime.—I am, Sir, your obed* ser*.

(Sig^d)   "PAT. DUFF."

EXTRACT LETTER.—ARCH^D DUNBAR, Duffus, to ALEX^R DUNBAR, Esq., Edinbro'.

29. *Feby.* 1764.

"It is long since I might have written you anent your unlucky friend at Abeⁿ whom I Dare say you are sorry for. But as the only gentleman of that Detestable Company (who had Courage or Humanity to go to the Street with the unhappy combatants) was Mr Byres, and he being kept in custody, and examined with others before your Criminal Court, . . . to say nothing till that was over, of which at this date I have not heard the issue. Wherefor let me know how the matter now stands. For if it shall appear that the other proud man Got but Fair Play, such as one Gentleman could expect from another, I shall have little doubt but that the Living man will come off by the interposition of Friends."

EXTRACT LETTER.—A. D. (ALEX^R DUNBAR), to ARCH^D DUNBAR, Esqr of Thunderton.

Dated from Elgin, Thursday Night.

"I examin'd him (Mr Sheriff), about Mayen and Leithhall, he says Leithhall gave the Lye, and Mayen gave a challange. Leithhall said he had no pistels. Mayen call'd for his Pistols and offer Leithhall one of them which he excepted of, they satt a good while after that, and the Pistols befor them on the Table, at last Leithhall went out and left his pistel, Mayen follow'd after, and caried both the pistols with him, then Byres went out, he says Byres is using all his intirst to have a Tryal immeadiately. and no Body can know the real Truth of the thing but him, he also says that they prevaricat as much about it at Aberdeen, as the doe here, but that most people is of opinion that Mayen gave Leithhall fair-play for his life, its tak'd that Stoneywood has sent Mayen to Gotenburgh."

FAMILY OF SMITH, OF GROTTHILL AND KING'S CRAMOND.

I. John Smyth, so the surname is uniformly spelt in the Registers at this period, merchant-burgess of Edinburgh, married Agnes Purves.

    1. Sir John.
    1. Geils or Egidia, married Sir William Gray of Pittendrum, see p. 111.
    2. Agnes, who married, first, 1617–1618, John Byres, I. of Coates, see p. 107, and secondly, the Revd James Reid, Minister of St Cuthbert's, Edinburgh—1630 to June 1634, when he died. (His father was John Reid, merchant-burgess of Edinburgh). Issue—
        1. William Reid, bap. 30. Jany. 1632, see p. 111.
        1. Agnes Reid.
        2. Margaret Reid.
        3. —— perhaps another daughter, married to John Johnston, merchant-burgess of Edinburgh, who may have been the descendant of Johnston of Coates, p. 101.

II. Sir John Smyth, of Grotthill, and King's Cramond, county Edinburgh, was Provost of the capital of Scotland, and many years its Member of Parliament.

Arms of Sir John. Azure a saltire couped, between three flames of fire, a bordure, or.

Thus, in a Funeral Escutcheon, but for his sister Giles Smith, wife of Sir William Gray, of Pittendrum, there are four flames instead of three, and the bordure is argent. Sir John Smyth Scottish represented Edinburgh in Parliament 1638 to 1663. His arms Arms. Vol. II., are also to be seen cut in stone on the house of Sir William Gray, p. 373. of Pittendrum, ancestor of the Lords Gray, who married his sister Egidia Smyth.

FAMILY OF SANDILANDS, OF CRAIBSTONE AND COTTON, IN THE COUNTY OF ABERDEEN.

COMPILED FROM A GENEALOGY WRITTEN ABOUT 1770.

"Justi ut sidera fulgent" (The righteous shine as the stars).

The surname of Sandilands is one of the most ancient in Scotland, and was assumed by the proprietors of the Barony of Sandilands, in the county of Lanark, as early as the reign of King Malcolm Canmore, who ascended the throne in the year 1057, about which period surnames at first became hereditary in this country. The chiefs of this name were the Barons of Sandilands in the county of Lanark, who afterwards became Barons of Calder, in the county of Edinburgh, and are now represented by the Lord Torphichen, whose descent is deduced from the royal family of Scotland, by the marriage of his ancestor, Sir James Sandilands, of Calder, Knight, with the Princess Jean, fifth daughter of Robert the Second.

The family of Craibstone and Cotton descend from

I. James Sandilands, who settled in Aberdeenshire about the year 1606 (a descendant of the Barons of Middlerig, in the county of Lanark, and of Bold, in the county of Peebles, who were very ancient cadets of the Barons of Sandilands, and were possessed of the lands above mentioned as early as the reign of King Malcolm the Fourth, who succeeded to the crown in 1153, from whom they were granted by charter to be held of the king), bought the lands of Craibstone, in Newhills parish. He was Doctor of Law, an Advocate before the Court of Session, and Commissary of Aberdeen. Besides other important offices which he held, he was for many years Clerk to the General Assemblies of the Church of Scotland, and appears to have been the first who was deprived of office for adhering to the measures of his sovereign King Charles I. James Sandilands m^d 1606 Catherine eldest dau. of Thomas Paterson, of Granton, in the Merse, merchant, of Edinburgh, by his wife Christian Nicolson, "of the family of Carnock, by whom he had four sons and two daughters,—the eldest son Thomas Sandilands, of Craibstone, m^d Margaret Cumming of Culter, on Deeside, and continued the family" of Craibstone. The 2^d son,

II. James Sandilands (born 1610, died 1650)—"a person of great worth, learning, and eloquence"—I, of Cotton, near Aberdeen. M⁴ 1640 Marjory, dau. of Bailie Alexander Burnett, of Countesswells (2ᵈ son to Sir Thomas Burnett, Bart., of Leys), merchant in Aberdeen. He was first Regent and thereafter Civilist of the King's College, and Town Clerk of Aberdeen ; and when King Charles II. was at Aberdeen, he received His Majesty with the magistrates, and upon his delivering to the King the keys of the town, he made a remarkable speech in Latin. The King took such notice of him on this occasion that on his Restoration he sent him a letter appointing him one of the Lords of Session, but he (unhappily) died a few days before the letter arrived. Issue, three sons and two daughters.

    1. Patrick, his heir.

    2. James, of Countesswells, Provost of Aberdeen. M⁴ first a dau. of the family of Arbuthnott, widow of a younger brother of Sir Thomas Burnett, Bart., of Leys, and 2ᵈˡʸ Ann, dau. of John Udny, of Newhills, and had issue.[1]

    3. Robert, rector of Spine, in Berkshire, died without issue.

    1. Jean, m⁴ John Moir, of Kermuck, afterwards of Stoneywood. See that family, p. 72.

    2. Rachel, m⁴ John Gordon, younger, of Fechill (" of the family of Straloch "), in the parish of Ellon, Aberdeenshire, and had issue one son and three daughters.

        1. Katherine Gordon (the youngest), m⁴ Bailie John Burnett, merchant in Aberdeen (commonly called " Bonnie John "), by whom with a dau., Margery Burnett, m⁴ to Patrick Turnbull, merchant, Aberdeen (a brother of Strathcathro in Angus), and had issue. She had an only son.

            1. James Burnett, merchant in Aberdeen, who m⁴ Isobel, dau. of John Black, merchant, of Bordeaux, by his wife, a dau. of Robert Gordon, of Hallhead, and of his wife, Isabel, 2ᵈ dau. of James Byres, of Aberdeen, merchant (see p. 118). Mrs. Isobel Black or Burnett was sister of Joseph Black,

---

[1] James Sandilands, of Countesswells, had by his 2ᵈ wife, Ann Udny, of Newhills, a dau., Martha Sandilands, m⁴ George Gordon, of Shillagreen (see p. 30), without issue.

M.D., the celebrated chemist. They had a numerous family, of which one son was Lieut.-Col. Joseph Burnett, of Gadgirth, in Ayrshire, getting that estate through marrying Margaret Steele the heiress thereof, whose eldest dau., Margaret Burnett, became, in 1834, the 2^d wife of her cousin-german, Gen. Byres, III. of Tonley (see p. 130), while a dau., Margaret Burnett, m^d 1770 Robert Byres, of Memil, &c. (see p. 118), and their son, Gen. Patrick Byres, m^d his cousin as above.

BURNETTS OF DALADIES.

Lyon Reg.,
1672-78.
I. John Burnett, of Daladies, descended of Leys (Kincardineshire), bears argent, three holly leaves, in chief vert, and a hunting horn in base sable, garnished gules, within a bordure counter componed of the second and first. M^d Agnes, dau. of Turnbull, of Strathcathro, his son,

II. John Burnett ("Bonnie John"), bailie and merchant of Aberdeen. M^d 1st a dau. of Paton, of Grandholme, their eld. son, John Burnett, b. 1704, also of Aberdeen, merchant, who m^d Theodosia Stuart, of Dens, from them the Burnett-Stuarts, of Dens and Crichie, are descended. John Burnett m^d 2dly Katherine Gordon, of Fechill, as before stated, and had a son,

Ibid.,
1672-8.
III. James Burnett, merchant in Aberdeen. M^d Isobel Black (see former page), and had a large family, of which one son was Col. Joseph Burnett, of Gadgirth, and a dau., Margaret Burnett, m^d 1770 Robert Byres, of Kincragie and Memel—see p. 118. Mr James Sandilands, of Craibstone, bears 1 and 4 argent, a bend counter-embattled, azure, 2 and 3 argent, a heart gules, on a chief azure, three mullets of the first.

Crest, a star issuing out of a crescent ; motto, as given.

III. Patrick Sandilands II., of Cotton. M^d 1st Margaret, dau.

of William Ord, of Cairnbee, in Fifeshire, by his wife, a dau. of Grahame of Fintray, by whom he had three sons and three daughters, viz. :—

1. Patrick, Sheriff of Aberdeen. M^d Barbara, dau. of William Cumine, of Pittulie (ancestor of Cumine of Rattray), in Aberdeenshire, and left no issue.
2. William, served in the navy. Died without issue.
3. George, III. of Cotton. Sold his family property, and settled in France as a wine factor, at Bordeaux. M^d 1721 Susanaa Palmer, an English merchant's daughter, and had issue.

1. Isabell, m^d William Black, advocate in Edinburgh, and had issue.
2. Jean, m^d 1704, Robert Byres, of Dublin. See p. 120.
3. Rachel, m^d James Dalgarno, of Aberdeen, merchant, and had issue.

Patrick Sandilands m^d secondly Magdalen Boyes, widow of Alexander Davidson of Newton, Aberdeenshire, and had an only daughter.

4. Margaret, m^d Thomas Paull, of Aberdeen, merchant, and had issue.

James Sandilands, III. of Craibstone (son of Thomas Sandilands, II. of Craibstone, and Margaret Cumming, of Culter—see p. 180). M^d for his 2^d wife Elizabeth, dau. of John Donaldson, of Hilton.

1. John, IV. of Craibstone. M^d Jean, dau. of Sir James Gordon, of Lesmoir, and had issue.
2. Alexander, whose only child is presently, 1770, Lady Torphichen.

1. Jean, m^d Sir William Johnstone, V., Bart., of that ilk, &c., and had issue.
2. Anne, m^d James Gordon, of Auchline, and had issue.
3. Elizabeth, m^d Thomas Mossman, advocate, Aberdeen. No issue.

DONALDSONS OF AUCHMULL, &c.

"Sub Cruce Lux" (Salvation through the Cross).

This family, doubtless a branch of the numerous and powerful Clan of MacDonald, were long settled in Aberdeenshire—one branch owned for a time the estate of Hilton in the parish of Ellon, and in the "Memoranda of the family of Forbes of Watertoune," printed at Aberdeen in 1857, at p. 57, John Donaldson of Hilton is mentioned in 1652—see p. 78. The Donaldsons of Kinnardie, on Devronside, in the county of Banff, were not, so far as I know, of the same stock, although I think the Donaldsons of Auchmull, in the parish of Newhills, Aberdeenshire (who for many years owned that property), were.

I. Robert Donaldson and Issobell Irvine were married on Tuesday, being the sixteenth day of Aprile 1695 years, by Mr Andrew Burnett, Minr. of Abd. at Cults House. (This Robert Donaldson was most probably son of John Donaldson and Isobel Leslie, whose initials are on outside, and names on fly-leaf, of Family Bible,[1] from which most of the following dates, &c., are taken.) His wife Isobell Irvine was a daughter of the Laird of Cults, a cadet of the ancient house of Drum. Robert Irvine of Cults was probably Mrs Donaldson's father.

I. Robert Donaldson and Issobell Irvine of Cults, had issue—

1. Robert, born, 21st, and bap. 26 Jany. 1696, by Dr William Blair. Godfathers, Mr Ro. Irvine, Cults, Mr Ro. Paterson, Commissary, Ro. Burnett of Elrick, Ro. Gordon of Stroloch, Ro. Bruce, Merct., Ro. Abercrombie, Merct. Died 23 Septr 1734.

2. John, born 9 June, 1697, and bap. by Dr Blair. Godfathers, Provost Sandilands, Mr John Stewart, John Bruice, John Gray, Bailzie, Jo. Anderson, and died 24 May 1698, and was buried beside his grandfather and grandmother.

3. James, his heir, born and bap. 24 March 1699, by Dr Blair.

[1] This Bible bears the names of "John Donaldson—Isobel Leslie, and motto, 'Sub Cruce Salus,' Anno Domini, 1694." Also, Feby. 16, 1695, Bethia Donaldson dyed, buried at the left syde of her Father's ston, &c.

Godfathers James Roland, Dishlair, eld James Milne,
Blairtoun, James Fyffe, Merct., James Bayly, Merct.,
James Mercer, Mercht.

4. Andrew, born 17 Feby. 1702.

1. Issobel, born 21 Sept and bap. 24 1700 by D Blair. Wit-
nesses, Alex Walker, provost, Geo. Davidson of Cairn-
brougie, James Robertson, M Gilbert Leslie, Mercht.
Name Mothers, Issobell Forbes, ye lady Auchnegat,
Issobell Irvin, w. to J. Robertson, Issobell Black, wife to
B. Ro. Cuming.

II. James Donaldson, M.D. of Auchmull, Physician in Aberdeen, m at Hilton, 5th Dec 1727, Katherine Gordon (who died
1755), daughter of John Gordon, M.D., of Hilton, near Old Aberdeen, and sister of James Gordon, M.D., of Hilton, who eventually
succeeded to the family property of Pitlurg (see Gordon of Pitlurg—Burke's Landed Gentry). Another sister of the last gentleman and of Mrs Donaldson, m Turner of Menie in the parish of
Belhelvie, Aberdeenshire. Issue—

1. Alexander, born 4 March 1731, his heir.
2. Andrew, born, 23 July 1732.
3. John, born 21 Dec 1734. Witnesses, John Burnet Turner
and John Rickhart, Auchnecant. Died 21 Jany. 1737,
buried next day under his great-grandfather's stone in the
churchyard.
4. James, born 13 June 1743, died 26 May 1744.
1. Margaret, born 12 Oct 1728.
2. Isobel, born 10 Dec 1737, bap. same day by M Keith.
Witnesses, Mrs Bell More and Bell McKell. Died 23
Aug 1738.
3. Katherine, born 7 Sept 1740.
4. Isobel, born 25 April 1745. Married in 1744 Cap John
Byres, R.E. (see Byres of Tonley, p. 125).

Dr James Donaldson, died 25 July 1761.

III. Alexander Donaldson, M.D.,[1] of Auchmull, married 3
Aug 1779, Hope, daughter of John Burnet of Elrick, and widow
of James Davidson of Midmar, both in Aberdeenshire.

[1] Several of this family were Professors of Medicine in Marischall College,
Aberdeen—1732. James Donaldson, II. of Auchmull—1754-55, Alexander
Donaldson.

Dr Alexander Donaldson died 19 May 1793.

The Lyon Register contains ten entries of arms for this name from 1672 onwards, all but one bearing the eagle and lymphad of Macdonald, and in some cases a descent from the Glencoe family being stated. In 1642 a Litera Prosapiæ under the Great Seal was issued in favour of Alexander Donaldson, M.D., son of Walter Donaldson, Professor of Philosophy at Sedan, tracing his descent, through five generations, from Donald Donaldson of Esslemond, designed baron, and Isabella Hay his wife, of the noble house of Errol.

Scottish Arms, p. 30.

Donaldson of Auchmull, or, an eagle displayed with two heads sable, beaked, and membered, gules, surmounted of a galley, of the second, flagged of the third, on a dexter cauton, argent, a sinister hand couped gules, all within a bordure of the last. Crest, a passion cross, gules. Motto, "Sub Cruce Lux." The Donaldsons of Hilton have similar arms, but a different crest and motto.

Lyon Register

INDEX.

A

2 B

2 C

M

2 F

CORRIGENDA.

Page 28, fourteenth line, *for* Jane *read* Jean.

   „ 48, from the seventh line of the text *delete* about.

   „ 56, from the first line *delete* David.

   „ 62, last line but one, *for* conveying *read* converging.

   „ 62,   „   *for* hyperbole *read* hyperbola.

   „ 65, from the second line *delete* " and of James VI."

   „ 65, seventh line, *for* John *read* Colin.

   „ 65, sixteenth line, *insert* Peter *before* Burnett.

   „ 66, twenty-third line, *for* Cattanch *read* Cattanach.

   „ 72, twelfth line, *for* Colton *read* Cotton.

   „ 85, fourth line from foot, *for* p. 87 *read* 88.

   „ 87, fourth line from foot, *insert* a comma between More and
        Baxter.

  „ 118, fourth line from foot, *for* Dr. John Black *read* Dr.
        Joseph Black.

CPSIA information can be obtained
at www.ICGtesting.com
Printed in the USA
LVHW040601291222
736094LV00001B/114